"A must-read book if you want a concise, easy to follow and informative guide to financial security."

Joni Revenna, host and producer of the
PBS-TV travel series, *Earth Trek*

"Finally, an easy to understand blueprint for financial success that provides honest answers and insight that both the individual investor and seasoned pro will be sure to benefit from."

Eric Schnell, business owner and former Wall Street executive

"Ken Marinace is helping people at all income levels to take control of their financial future."

Les Dubow, real estate investor and
Deputy District Attorney, San Diego County

"At last, a book about personal financial independence that is easy to read, understand and implement."

Victor Benoun, president, *The Mortgage Source, Inc.*,
and author of *Your Castle, No Hassle*

A Step-by-Step Guide to Financial Bli$$

By Ken Marinace, CFP

with Vera Tweed

Tweedmedia
Los Angeles, California

Printed in the United States of America

ISBN 0-9678733-0-4

Library of Congress Control Number 2002094446

Certified Financial Planner™ and CFP™ are registered trademarks of the Certified Financial Planner Board of Standards.

Material in this book is meant for general illustration and/or informational purposes only and it is not to be construed as tax, legal, or investment advice. Although the information has been gathered from sources deemed reliable, please note that individual situations can vary, therefore, the information should be relied upon when coordinated with individual professional advice. This material is not an offer to sell, nor is it a solicitation of an offer to buy any security. The publisher is not engaged in rendering legal, tax or accounting advice.

Design by Donna Schmidt

Published by
Tweedmedia
Los Angeles, CA
Tel: 310-943-1555
Fax: 310-943-1755
Email: info@tweedmedia.com

contents

Preface

I am delighted to give you the opportunity to take advantage of my career as a financial planner, which began in 1967. While the world has changed dramatically over these many years, the fundamentals for achieving financial independence remain the same. I believe this book can be a great help to those who create a strategy, a lifestyle, a discipline — if you will — based on the ideas and planning considerations that appear in these pages. These concepts have been tested and proven to work well over time.

My goal here is to give you the confidence that you can indeed achieve financial bliss. By financial bliss, I am talking about security, a worry-free financial future, and the means by which to live the life of your dreams.

As an eighteen-year-old working on Wall Street and attending college at night, I would take New York City's elevated IRT Line No. 7 twice each day. As the train traveled through Long Island City, it passed many warehouses and factories belonging to a company called Eagle Electric Manufacturing. In each location, on a sign beneath the company name, a slogan read: "Perfection is Not an Accident." Passing these buildings (several of them still exist today) and seeing this message literally thousands of times inspired me and helped create, for me, a sort of doctrine as to how I would attempt to conduct my business life. That same principle also became the framework for concepts that I would ultimately share with my clients to help them take charge of their financial future.

Around 1965, in his recording, "Sinatra: A Man and His Music," that American icon reflected on how he accounted for his great musical successes over so many years: "I make every record as if it will be the last song I ever sing."

These anecdotes and aphorisms have helped me understand the effort and attention to detail that ensure success. While true perfection is unattainable, we can be and need to be inspired to get the most out of life and our financial resources by setting goals and objectives, and, most importantly, monitoring our results objectively along the way to be certain we're still on track.

Hopefully, the chapters ahead will provide a roadmap for the start of a successful financial journey that will last as long as you live.

chapter 1

Adopting a New Perspective

Money has a way of disappearing. Where does it go? If you subscribe to conspiracies, the "other sock" theory may be plausible. Socks enter the laundry basket in pairs, but by the time they exit the dryer, some of their mates are inevitably MIA. Perhaps money is naturally drawn to the same, secret world that harbors those missing socks?

Despite the risk of disappointing you, I have to be honest. Even though my experience as a financial planning professional spans more than 30 years, I don't possess a shred of insider information about a clandestine world filled with orphaned socks and lost currency.

Now that I've revealed my ignorance, you may be wondering how I can help you become the master of your own money. The fact is, if you know your financial goals, follow your money closely enough and make conscious decisions about where it goes, it doesn't have a chance to disappear into some illusive netherworld. Instead, it grows and helps you to achieve those things you care about in life. In essence, that's what financial planning is all about, but it's easier said than done.

This book covers a sequence of steps that, if implemented, will improve your financial future. Some of the actions I recommend may seem too obvious to merit mention, while others may seem unrealistically cumbersome or complex. I invite you to keep an open mind. Realize that if managing money was easy, most people would have more than they know what to do with.

Dealing with our own preconceptions is often the most difficult aspect of improving our financial circumstances. Each one of us has certain ideas about money, both about earning it and spending it. Some people can't see any way to earn more; others can't fathom how to spend less. In every situation, there are choices, but being human, we don't necessarily see all the options that exist.

I invite you to look at the material in this and the following chapters from a practical perspective, to ask yourself how you can put the information to use and to question your own preconceptions along the way. If something seems completely impractical, at least give it the benefit of the doubt. Then, if it still seems silly or impossible, let me know.

I've tried my best to distill what I've learned, through formal training and by working with several thousand people over the years, and to focus on the key factors that make the difference between financial success and failure. I hope that you use the information to move closer to your goals.

Success vs. Failure

There is an old adage: People don't plan to fail, but they do fail to plan. All too often, planning is viewed as a luxury to be indulged in only when there is money "left over." Sadly, it's unlikely that such a day will magically dawn, no matter how hard anyone works or how much income increases.

Many people think they only need to earn more; then, managing money would be easy. Yet, it is not uncommon for two individuals, or families, with similar incomes and obligations, to be in very different financial positions. The assets of one may be as large as or larger than the liabilities of the other.

Very often, as income grows, spending increases even more.

When America experienced a recession in 1991, people were spending 12.6 percent of their net income on personal debt (in addition to mortgage and car payments). After a decade that saw some of the most impressive economic growth during the twentieth century, the debt level had risen to 14.1 percent. The increase in debt outpaced rising salaries.

The proliferation of credit cards has been a key driver of mounting debt because charging purchases changes the way we view spending. An experiment by two professors at the Massachusetts Institute of Technology illustrates the point. The professors held an auction for tickets to a Boston Celtics basketball game, dividing the bidders into two randomly selected groups: Those in one group could pay with a credit card, while the others had to pay cash. Bids from the credit-card group were twice as high as bids from the cash-only group.

So how do you tame the wild bronco disguised as a slim, wallet-sized piece of plastic? Start by recognizing that financial planning is an essential activity that starts with setting goals.

Being a very personal matter, goals can vary widely from one individual to another. Frequently, financial goals include:

- sending children to college
- buying a home or moving up to a larger home
- retiring comfortably
- going back to college
- traveling
- buying a vacation property
- starting a business
- buying rental property
- eliminating debt.

There are also ongoing goals, which add up to maintaining a certain standard of living or lifestyle. This category includes:

- the type of neighborhood we live in
- how we furnish our house
- the type of car we drive
- how we vacation
- the way we dress
- where and how we shop
- what we do for entertainment
- how often we eat out and the types of restaurants we frequent
- the style in which we entertain family and friends
- sports or hobbies.

Often, lifestyle-related expenses are such that there isn't enough left over to plan for anything else. I'm not saying that you shouldn't enjoy life. However, many financial decisions are based on impulse, force of habit or preconceived notions, rather than being conscious choices, resulting in less than ideal consequences. The absence of clear goals is a basic problem, because if you don't know what you are trying to accomplish, it's virtually impossible to make smart decisions – much like sailing without a compass.

Take a moment to identify your own goals and write them down. The second part is just as important as the first, so don't skimp on it. Use a blank notebook, your computer or the checklist at right. I don't recommend using the back of an envelope, but if you must, once you've finished writing, stick the envelope on your refrigerator or in some other very prominent place. Your goals are a key to your success, and the paper they're recorded on should be treated with respect.

Opting for Success

Envisioning a rosy future is one thing, you may be thinking, but achieving it is a different matter. You're absolutely right. Part of the challenge stems from our culture, which elevates

goals

_____

_____

_____

_____

_____

_____

_____

_____

_____

_____

_____

_____

shopping to a noble pastime. While shopping has its place, the idea of spending to save is not a viable financial strategy. A "sale," in the real world, promotes more spending by encouraging purchases that would never have been made at the regular price. The good news is that there are some time-tested ways to bring about a better financial situation for you and those you care about.

Once you've established your goals, finding out where your money is going is the next step. Although that may seem pretty straightforward, it isn't always an easy task. You don't have to find orphaned socks, but you do have to develop some keen tracking skills.

In classic Western movies, the sheriff chasing bank robbers often enlisted the help of a native guide who knew the terrain, examined footprints and broken twigs, and put his trained ear to the ground to find the path traveled by outlaws. The process worked well, with the robbers being arrested within an hour or so. As you might expect, the bad guys – disappearing dollars in this case — are harder to catch in real life.

It may seem odd to compare chasing bank robbers with the process of analyzing one's cash flow. In the old Westerns, both sheriffs and guides were brave and strong, standing up to mighty fists and dodging flying bullets. Surely, they would have sneered at the prospect of crunching numbers. Or would they?

In today's world, tracking your money is as important a survival skill as catching outlaws was in the Wild West (although admittedly, galloping after bank robbers looks much more exciting). One problem is that record keeping and number crunching don't seem to provide any instant reward, but you might consider these activities akin to getting in the saddle because without an accurate picture of where you stand, you really can't embark on the journey to a wealthier place.

Footprints and Broken Twigs

When professional financial planners start working with clients, one of the first things they do is a "cash flow analysis." Performing a similar function to footprints and broken twigs, a cash flow statement lists every dollar of income and every expense. Hopefully, the income is greater than the expenses, but as you probably know, that isn't always the case.

To start tracking money coming in and going out, you need to have records. To track income, you should have records of every source of money you receive, including those below. You

income sources*

Salary
Commissions
Bonuses
Tax refunds
Child support
Alimony
Business or self-employment income
Dividends
Interest earned
Capital gains
Rent payments received
Trust income
Social Security income
Pension
Royalties
Residuals
Other

*The Appendix contains an Income Tracking Worksheet and an Expense Tracking Worksheet, which you can copy and use to analyze your own cash flow on an ongoing basis. Or, you may prefer to use your computer and input your figures into a spreadsheet or financial management program that will do the math for you. Later chapters discuss income and expenses in more detail.

can use this format or invent one that works better for your own situation, but the important thing is to have a record. If you have a mate, his or her income in all these categories should also be listed.

Expenses are the other side of the cash flow picture. If you don't already keep a running record of where your money goes each month, you can use the following list as a guide.

expenses

Home mortgage or rent
Second mortgage, if any
Home equity loan or credit line
Utilities: electricity
Utilities: gas
Utilities: other
Telephone
Cable or satellite TV services
Internet services
Property taxes
Homeowners or renters insurance
Car loan or lease payments
Car repairs/maintenance
Gas
Toll or other commuting fees
Insurance: car
Insurance: health
Insurance: life
Insurance: disability
Insurance: long term care
Insurance: other
Medical costs, out of pocket
Dental costs
Groceries

more expenses

Dining out
Other entertainment
Child care
School tuition
College tuition
Other educational costs
Clothing
Dry cleaning
Vacations
Gifts, including birthdays, anniversaries and Christmas/Chanukah
Income taxes: federal
Employment taxes
Income taxes: state
Business or other taxes
Sports or hobbies
401k or IRA contributions
Charitable contributions
Credit card payments
Other loan payments
Savings
Emergency fund
Other

You may already know whether your income or expenses are greater. If not, I encourage you to do the math; at least do enough calculations to determine if the total is a positive or negative amount. If you seem to make more than you spend but never have any money left over, realize that there's some work ahead to locate those elusive dollars. And if the process of compiling all this information seems overwhelming, keep reading, because I'll address the whole subject in more detail throughout the rest of the book.

Chapter 2, Getting Paid What You're Worth, and Chapter 3, Planning To Earn More, explore how you can increase your income. Chapter 4, Spending Wisely, looks at expenses in more detail and provides some practical ways to control spending without feeling deprived. Chapter 5, Use and Abuse of Debt, includes a worksheet to track the cost of debt, so if you're setting up a filing system, make sure your credit card bills and loan documents are included.

The remaining chapters in this book cover other basic elements of managing your money in a way that gives you greater financial control and brings you closer to your goals, including preserving your assets, minimizing taxes, keeping money in the best places, investing wisely, retiring comfortably, discussing financial issues with children and parents, leaving a legacy, and working with financial professionals.

Traditionally, financial planners seek clients with substantial assets; the professional's function is to preserve and grow that wealth. Consequently, professional planners usually serve those who have already been exceptionally successful (or lucky). Although the number of such people grows more rapidly in this country than anywhere else on earth, it still represents only a tiny minority of the U.S. population.

Aside from working with the financial minority, I would like to see more Americans be financially secure, less dependent on debt and more in control of their financial future. The basic principles that enable the wealthy to get wealthier can be used by anyone to significantly improve financial circumstances. And that's what this book is about — values and strategies that you can use to improve your personal financial situation.

chapter 2

Getting Paid
What You're Worth

November 1999: A 29-year-old office manager whose annual salary is $28,000 has a net worth of over $1 million, all accumulated during the past three years. You might assume — incorrectly — that she's the lucky beneficiary of a wealthy relative. In fact, she works for a small but rapidly growing software company in Silicon Valley, which, like its competitors, offers all of its employees stock options — and that's how she made her million.

Several hundred miles south, a 54-year-old hardware store sales clerk earns the same salary but no stock options. He spent 25 years building his million, working as an aerospace engineer, then lost his job nearly a decade ago with thousands of other "secure" professionals in defense-related industries who were uprooted after the end of the cold war. He watched his assets shrink rapidly during the four years he looked for another engineering job in a market glutted with professionals in the same situation. Finally, he and his wife moved to a much smaller home, and both accepted a new, scaled-down lifestyle that includes his job at the hardware store.

The technology world doesn't always offer expected earnings, either. Many young entrepreneurs in Internet-related businesses went from riches to rags and moved in with their parents after the "dot com" bubble burst. And after Enron stock plummeted, former employees who had lost their life savings were a frequent topic of financial news reports.

A rapid evolution of technology, global competition and dramatic corporate restructuring and downsizing have brought about a new world of business, one in which the traditional concept of "job security" has ceased to exist. A "good education" and a "good job" with a "good company" no longer guarantees a secure income. Instead, a whole new working world has emerged, with new opportunities as well as pitfalls.

Entrepreneurs have always had to deal with the ebb and flow of the marketplace, but the successful ones today have to be more astute in tracking and predicting changes and adjusting their strategies accordingly. And now, every working person has to understand the business world around them and to manage their own careers. In fact, successful planning for a business or for your career (in the role of employee) are more similar today than at any time in history. Both require accurate perception of the marketplace.

Important Trends

Would you refuse more income if it was offered to you? You may be doing just that, indirectly, because neither formal education nor on-the-job training builds skill in how to maximize your own earning potential. Having a good grasp of what's considered valuable in the business world, now and in the foreseeable future, is a basic requirement for getting paid every penny you're worth.

Education alone doesn't guarantee a good livelihood, but it's becoming a requirement in more and more jobs. In 2000, jobs that required a college degree or other post-secondary education made up 29 percent of America's total, but such jobs will account for 42 percent of new job growth between 2000 and 2010, according to the Bureau of Labor Statistics (BLS).

Service industries that require minimal education, and pay the lowest wages, will be the another big growth area. These two opposite ends of the education and income spectrum are expected to make up more than half the total job growth between 2000 and 2010.

In addition, the trends in the charts aren't the only ones in America's workplace, but they have an impact on your paycheck.

10 industries with the fastest wage and salary employment growth, 2000-2010

Computer and data processing services
Residential care
Health services
Cable and pay television services
Personnel supply services
Warehousing and storage
Water and sanitation
Miscellaneous business services
Miscellaneous equipment rental and leasing
Management and public relations

10 fastest-growing occupations, 2000-2010

Computer software engineers, applications
Computer support specialists
Computer software engineers, systems software
Network and computer systems administrators
Network systems and data communications analysts
Desktop publishers
Database administrators
Personal and home-care aides
Computer systems analysts
Medical assistants

Source: Bureau of Labor Statistics

Trend #1: Technology

If we are to believe the government's projections, eight of the ten fastest-growing occupations fall under the "information technology" umbrella. This doesn't mean you have to become a computer specialist to maximize your earnings. But whatever your field, chances are that knowledge of technology could make you more efficient, more employable, or just plain old richer.

Consider car sales. If you had walked into a car lot a few years ago and told the sales team that people would buy a lot of cars using their computers instead of shopping in the lot, they probably would have laughed. But Autobytel, one online car-buying service that refers site users to local car dealers, accounted for one in every twenty dollars spent on new cars in 2001. If you were the first salesperson in a dealership to figure out how to tap into the online market and you cornered it (while everyone else scoffed at the idea), you'd probably be a lot richer by now.

You may think the car sales idea would have been too complex for one salesperson to develop — not so. Anyone who was thinking while using the Internet as early as 1995 (when Autobytel started) could see that online car sales were going to happen. Another point was obvious too: car dealers weren't plugged in. So if a prospect wanted to ask questions about a car via email, it was very difficult to find someone to answer.

In essence, a car salesperson would have had to convince his or her employer to spend about $50 for a modem setup, another $20 per month for an Internet account, and to allow time to answer all email from prospects. But because most people tend to resist new ideas, selling the concept to the boss could be the toughest pitch any car salesperson ever made. No doubt, the opportunity probably still exists in some car lots today.

What if technology poses a real danger? What if you're a bank teller counting the days before another ATM replaces you? Consider finding out what technology you need to know to increase your foothold and earning power within the banking industry. If you've held your position for a while, you may be able to get training paid by the bank, either in-house or at a local college. If you ask enough people within the organization, you may get more than free computer training; someone may notice you have some foresight and initiative — that you're thinking creatively — which brings up another trend.

Trend #2: Creative Thinking and Communication Skills

Regardless of the job or its position on a company ladder, these two abilities — to think creatively and to communicate well — are assets today's business world values very highly. They're also vital for any self-employed person.

Creative thinking falls into two main categories: identifying and solving problems and recognizing and exploiting opportunities for a company, such as tapping into new markets. "Thinking outside the box" is a phrase often used to describe this trait. The "box" in this context is an old way of thinking: "Good" employees followed directions without question, carried the party line and generally didn't speak unless spoken to. That attitude isn't worth much today, because if everyone agrees with the status quo, new ground can't be broken and the company can't grow. One of the reasons companies hire outside consultants is to get a fresh perspective.

Communication skills, both written and verbal, have become vital for doing anything from working in teams with people from other disciplines to "selling" an executive or a whole committee of them on a better way to do things. Communication is a natural accomplice of creative thinking — it's what you have to do to get other people to agree with you about how to solve the problems or exploit the opportunities.

If any of this seems even remotely unbelievable, consider a world like accounting, where number crunching is the basic activity — or so it seems. In the real world of finance, communication and creativity are paramount. A career planning guide from one of the country's largest staffing companies makes this point:

"Today, accounting and finance professionals are being asked to do more: to be strategic thinkers and provide creative solutions on everything from marketing strategy to product development. To be successful, you will need to be proficient in communicating ideas through written and verbal presentations. Future performance reviews will be based on the ability to analyze information and situations and make decisions that drive the business rather than the ability to measure the business."

In other words, the skills to crunch numbers are taken for granted, but the real value of an accounting professional lies in his or her ability to envision ways (think creatively) to make the company more successful. And it doesn't stop there: constructive ideas have to be sold to others in management, which is why the communication skills are so important.

What about jobs below the management ranks, like the secretary? The old stereotype of a woman with limited skills and intellect, meekly following the boss's orders, may still get some laughs in a few sitcoms, but it doesn't reflect the real world too well. The job title has changed to "administrative assistant," "executive assistant" or just "assistant." And the profile has changed dramatically too: many assistants are very well educated; many are male; and most are highly skilled.

A survey of 2,000 classified want ads in major North American cities, by The Dartnell Corporation's Institute of Business Research and its *From 9 to 5* newsletter, showed employers are increasingly looking for support staff with skills that used to be considered managerial. In addition to basic computer skills such as word processing and spreadsheets, the survey found a growing demand for:

- project management
- event planning
- ability to give presentations
- personality traits such as "energetic, upbeat, positive and can-do"
- knowledge of computer databases.

Salaries ranged from $12,480 to $65,000. Although these are influenced by geography (New York City and Memphis, TN, offered the most money), the managerial traits definitely command more compensation across the boards. And compensation is the other key trend to keep in mind.

Trend #3: Performance-Based Compensation

The old "box" had some problems. Aside from the fact that it's difficult to gain a high level of personal satisfaction in a "be seen and not heard" environment, the system wasn't designed to reward an individual's achievements or contributions to a company's success. As a result, earning power had a predefined ceiling.

In contrast, today's compensation is being built around individual and overall company performance. Although performance-based bonuses are not new for senior executives, their application to rank-and-file employees is a new and growing trend.

Buck Consultants, an international human resources consulting firm, does an annual Compensation Budget Survey on Fortune 1000 companies. As early as 1998, Buck discovered a sharp rise in bonus programs for employees below the executive level. Over 73 percent of survey respondents paid bonuses to salaried employees, and nearly 40 percent paid bonuses to hourly-wage earners. In addition, some companies offer performance incentives to teams of employees who work on special projects.

If you can see the glass as half full (squint if you have to), today's business climate offers far greater earning potential than ever before.

Making Your Income Plan

As with any plan, the goals you have set the direction. You may want to change your lifestyle for reasons that bear no relationship to how much you earn. You may want to move from a fast-paced city life to a more serene rural area; you may want to change your occupation because you've always dreamed of doing something completely different; or you may want to switch from a traditional job to a home business because you'd like to spend more time with your family. All these are key factors to keep in mind. However, my focus here is to see how you can maximize your income.

The way of living that is important to you is equally important in your income plan, but in considering making changes, keep in mind some advice from a career expert. John Challenger, executive vice president of a leading outplacement firm, Challenger, Gray & Christmas, has assisted many seasoned professionals in repackaging themselves successfully for new positions. He cautions: "I see a lot of people damaging their financial security by trying to change their careers. After ten or fifteen years, people sometimes get tired or upset with what they do and want to change course, but if you move into a completely different field, you'll be starting at entry level."

Does this mean that you have to keep doing exactly what you do, in the same type of environment, no matter what? Not necessarily. "You can certainly change industries," says Challenger. "Let's say you're a human resources professional but you've always wanted to work in advertising. You could certainly move into the advertising world and retain your earning power — as long as you still work in human resources." The industry and culture of your employer could have a big impact on how well you work, so moving to a company that is much more in line with your own interests might lead to a much more productive, and better compensated, you.

Challenger has also seen people wanting to move from the corporate world into their own business, without really understanding what they would have to do. "They want to become an entrepreneur and don't realize they're buying a sales job. Starting your own business is basically being a salesperson for half or more of your working hours," he says.

As always, there are exceptions to the rule, but they are exceptions. An account executive moved from a high-pressure job with a leading Chicago advertising agency to an idyllic farmhouse in rural Maine and runs his own successful small agency from his country home. Right after the move, his income dropped but not too drastically, and after a couple of years, he's earning at least as much as he would have in his old job. In addition to being highly skilled in the creative areas of marketing and advertising, he is also very good at developing new clients.

You may know of similar successes yourself, and perhaps you are part of the minority of the population with good entrepreneurial instincts and sales skills. However, if you aren't but long for a less structured work schedule or prefer to work from home, keep in mind that companies today are much more flexible with schedules and that telecommuting is a growing trend. Most telecommuting jobs go to existing employees of companies, rather than new hires, so it's definitely worth investigating with your current employer.

In the income planning steps in this and the next chapter, I focus on looking at your existing occupation and skills and seeing how you can increase your earning power. Following this process will give you a picture of your strong and weak points.

Taking Stock of Your Assets

Your knowledge is what you trade for compensation in various forms: cash, employee benefits such as health insurance and retirement plans, and sometimes for equity in a company.

The knowledge you have, whether through formal education, work experience or informal study, is the first thing to assess in making a plan. Once that's done, you can take a look at whether there are better ways and avenues to market your own assets for a higher level of compensation, or whether you will need to build more assets to earn more, such as by gaining additional skills.

I've created a worksheet as a guide. Make sure that you include all the knowledge that may in any way influence your value in the workplace, keeping in mind the key trends in business. It's quite possible that you possess some very valuable assets that you've never considered relevant to your career. Hopefully, this exercise will help you identify some hidden pots of gold.

Once you've filled in the worksheet, you should be able to see if you have unused skills — if you have skills with a high score and checkmarks in the "never" or "rarely" columns. On the other hand, if you scored pretty low on many of the skill areas, you have some learning to do.

Appraising Your Own Market Value

This step is similar to pricing a home: you look at comparable properties in the same or similar neighborhoods and see what they sold for recently. It may be a bit more complex to determine what's a comparable property, i.e., your personal package of skills and knowledge, and the process definitely requires some research.

The quickest and easiest way to do your most basic homework is on the Internet. It isn't the only place you'll have to

asset inventory worksheet

For each of the following categories, rate your own level of knowledge on a scale of 1 to 10, with 10 being the highest. Then, put a check mark in the Application column that applies.

Area of skill	Degree of knowledge (rate from 1 to 10)	Application in business: I use this knowledge:			
		Never	Rarely	Sometimes	Always
Professional skills (list and rate each one)					
Relevant technology (list and rate each type of software, hardware or other specific skills)					
Creative thinking: problem solving					
Creative thinking: seeing opportunities					
Written communication					
Verbal communication					
"Selling" an idea to others					
Managing projects					
Familiarity with your industry					
Familiarity with competitors in your industry					
Familiarity with related industries					

look, but it's the best starting point. Career planning and job sites are growing like wildfire, and so is the quality of their content. It's estimated that there are over 100,000 job sites online, having grown from about 500 in 1995.

If the sheer numbers are daunting, rest assured that you'll never need to look at most of them. A few key sites contain just about all the information you would ever want, either at the site itself or through links to whatever else you're looking for — and we've summarized these in this and the next chapter.

However, if you'd really rather not use a computer at all, recognize that you will be depriving yourself of the most economical and efficient research tool there is for managing your career or business effectively. I'll try to give alternative information sources, but you will spend both time and money needlessly if you avoid the online world. And, quite frankly, by refusing to use what has become a basic business tool today, your chances of increasing your income decrease proportionally. (By the way, online research is also the most efficient for investment information.)

To get a realistic idea of your earning power, you need to look at some income surveys to get an overall picture of what people with your set of skills and experience are getting paid. The figures could represent a salary or fees for services you provide as a self-employed individual. If you are self-employed, it's also useful to see what employees performing your services get paid.

If you own a business, figure out what jobs you perform, such as president or CEO, perhaps sales manager or even sales rep — whatever you actually do. By comparing what you get paid for each of those jobs to others in the same occupation, you'll find out how much business ownership is actually paying off. Some business owners find they own a badly paid sales job. Others are delighted to discover how profitable their business really is.

As you collect salary information for your existing set of skills, it's a good idea to peek a little higher up at the next level — who gets paid a bit more, and what their job entails that yours doesn't. I'll be looking at that in more detail in the next chapter, but it's a good idea to keep your eyes open from the start.

Try these three steps to gather information about compensation for what you do:

1 | Check BLS surveys.

Start with salary and wage surveys by the BLS, Office of Compensation Levels and Trends. The information is available on the Internet at the BLS web site, by fax and in libraries (see Resources at end of chapter). Most of these surveys give a median (smack in the middle between the highest and lowest) income for the whole country and are a good basic reference point. Some are compiled by geographic area and give ranges of incomes by occupation. Due to the sheer volume of figures BLS compiles, these surveys will not give you all the detail you need — such as differences from one industry to another, bonuses, incentives and various employee benefit packages. However, it's a very good way to get a broad perspective on your field, and there are no fees.

2 | Explore the private sector.

For more detailed surveys, look in the private sector. Professional associations periodically do more detailed analyses of compensation, both for employees and independent contractors. The research results, and ongoing reports about compensation trends, are generally published in industry trade magazines or as special reports. They often include breakdowns by geography and other factors that will help you compare your earnings to others' more accurately. You can also call professional associations and ask where to find this information. If you're not sure where to find these organizations, search on the Internet or your local library can help.

3 | Talk to people in the know.

For a real grass-roots perspective, talk to people who know about compensation in your field and look at job listings — many of them give salary ranges and descriptions of other benefits. People to ask would include anyone you know who does work similar to yours or works in human resources or management in your field. Headhunters who place people in your occupation are also a very good source of information, and it's worth spending some time with the ones who know your field. When you look at employment ads, look for names of agencies that advertise appealing jobs. And whenever you talk to anyone, ask about longer-term income prospects, too.

Once you've gathered your information, you should be able to see how your compensation compares. You may have discovered opportunities in this process, or you may feel disappointed because it seems like you're at a dead end. Or maybe you feel pretty confident that you could increase your income but don't have a specific plan yet.

Recognize that you just did the first step — an appraisal of the "house" you've been building throughout your working years. You've set the stage to look for better offers or maybe spruce up the property by adding some skills to increase your earning power. And you're ready for the next planning step.

resources

Bureau of Labor Statistics Web site: http://stats.bls.gov
Lists comprehensive trend, earnings and benefit information for over 700 occupations nationally and regionally.

Libraries All BLS information is available in federal depository libraries throughout the country. Check with your local library to find the one nearest you.

Wageweb www.wageweb.com
Lists average compensation and bonuses for over 150 occupations in the fields of human resources, administration, finance, information management, engineering, healthcare, manufacturing, sales and marketing. Job descriptions for each occupation surveyed will be helpful for your comparison.

Other Resources
Many of the career sites summarized in the next chapter contain information about salaries and professional associations.

chapter 3

Planning To Earn More

I f you're not quite sure how you ended up doing what you do for a living, you're not alone. Only 32 percent of working adults made a conscious plan to be in their current job or career, according to a survey by the National Career Development Association, and 72 percent would find out more about career options if they were starting over. Luckily, it's never too late to start planning effectively.

If you completed the asset inventory in the previous chapter and appraised your market value, you're probably in one or more of the following situations:

- You're basically doing fine, earning your fair market value, and you're content with your career. If you think you don't need to do anything to improve your situation, you may be right for the moment. However, if your after-tax income doesn't increase by more than inflation, for the rest of your working life, you won't have a secure future. Understanding how to keep increasing your value in the workaday world by continually increasing your skills and marketing yourself is the only guarantee of income security in the longer term.
- You seem to be earning less than the going rate in your geographical area. You may be able to negotiate better compensation from your current employer or start looking elsewhere. In either case, marketing is your next step.
- You're getting paid fairly for what you do, but your job

doesn't offer opportunities for you to use valuable skills that are worth more in today's marketplace. It's possible that your employer may have other positions that would allow you to do more and get paid accordingly. Or, you may have to explore other possibilities. In both scenarios, marketing is called for right away.

- You need more skills to command a higher income. Once you've identified what type of competence you need to develop — whether it means taking a computer course or improving your verbal, writing or problem-solving skills — if you take action by learning, then marketing yourself, you'll be on your way.

- You seem to be at a dead end because your skills simply don't command sufficient income, and you may also lack career direction. It's time for an overhaul, which will include setting goals, learning the necessary skills and marketing the new professional you.

Regardless of your current situation, you can't get away from two key ingredients for ongoing professional success: marketing yourself and making learning an ongoing part of your life. Which factor is more important right now depends on your personal circumstances.

Learning

If you're old enough, you probably grew up with the idea that learning ends when you graduate from school or college and get a job. Now, thinking that way is like betting all your assets (right down to the clothes on your back) on the worst horse in the race.

"If you're going to be successful, you're never going to stop learning," says Norma Kent, spokesperson for the American Association of Community Colleges (AACC). "You can't take any job for granted," says Kent, "because some jobs are always disappearing, because of mergers, new technology or for whatever reason. At the same time, demand for other jobs is growing."

The AACC has found that 20 to 25 percent of community college enrollees in urban areas already have bachelors, masters or doctorate degrees, and the percentage of such students is steadily rising. Some of these college graduates take a single course to learn a new type of software, while others enroll in much longer programs because they need training that wasn't part of their college curriculum.

Community colleges today offer the most economical way not only to learn specific job-related skills, but also to get just about any information you may need to get your career on a better track or start building a new one. If you're not sure of the direction you should follow, college assessment offices can help by testing your aptitude in various areas and counseling to match your skills and interests with a career that fits, as well as providing information about education and financial aid. Some community colleges also have special programs, for example, for women or for anyone wanting to start their own business.

The growth of the Internet has made it much easier to find out what education is required in different professions, where it is offered, how much it costs and what financial aid is available. One Web site, courtesy of the federal government, America's Learning Exchange (see Resources), is a central point for mining this information. If you don't have Internet access, you can access the site at many community colleges or libraries, for no cost.

Four-year colleges also have extension or continuing education departments with an enormous variety of courses, some specifically tailored to help you revamp or enhance your career, others geared for specialized knowledge in a given field. One of the largest of these, University of California Los Angeles (UCLA) Extension (see Resources), offers over 70 courses online plus hundreds of others on Los Angeles area campuses. Other cities have similar institutions.

UCLA Extension offers both certificate programs (for which financial aid is available) and individual courses. Subjects cover many areas, including computer applications, business management, language skills, engineering and entertainment professions. Some writing courses, for example, focus on effective business reports or technical manuals, while others deal with creative writing. If you aim for a degree or certificate program at an accredited post-secondary school, some financial aid may be available.

Keep in mind that formal education isn't the only way to learn. Professional associations, trade magazines, conferences, employer-sponsored training seminars — all these offer valuable information. If you don't know where to find them, head for the reference desk at your local library and check with your employer about in-house programs or training for which you can be reimbursed.

If communication is something you really need to improve, a very economical way is by becoming a member of a Toastmasters Club, founded with the aim of helping people to speak more effectively. There are over 8,000 of these clubs around the country, half of them sponsored by employers. And if there isn't one near you, you can start one by contacting Toastmasters World Headquarters (see Resources).

All in all, no matter what type of education you need, it's safe to assume that you can find it for a reasonable cost or, in some cases, no cost. Taking advantage of the resources around you can mean the difference between a stagnant or insecure career or a successful and rewarding one.

Marketing

Every time I meet with a prospective new client, I go through the same process a job applicant experiences in that crucial first interview. But unlike many job applicants who dread the thought, I consider it a vital and enjoyable part of my profession. True, I am interviewing to get hired as a financial planner, and my prospects are checking me out, but it's a two-way street. I am also assessing the prospective clients, to see if I am the right choice of professional for them. If, and only if, I think I'm right for them, I demonstrate how I can do the job of improving their financial future — right there, in that first interview. (Naturally, "improving" is based on the client's needs and goals, which are unique in each situation.)

My approach essentially parallels the advice of career expert Nick Corcodilos. A former headhunter and author of *Ask the Headhunter: Reinventing the Interview to Win the Job,* Corcodilos also has a Web site I highly recommend (see Resources). He points out that mailing out hundreds of resumes or having lots of job interviews doesn't get results.

Attitude is the most critical element, according to Corcodilos — and I agree, completely. (By the way, I see things from both ends of the hiring process, since I hire employees as well as get hired by my clients). "Most job hunters project the attitude 'I'm looking for a job' rather than 'I'm here to do the work you need to have done,'" he says; "There is a big difference between looking to GET a job, and offering to DO a job."

"When you start searching for a new job," says Corcodilos, "place a renewed emphasis on your work and your ability to do it. THAT's what yields a job offer — not your resume or clever answers to the Top Ten Interview Questions." So what exactly do you do? "Start by understanding how your skills can profit a particular business," he says; "If you can't explain this to a prospective employer, why should he or she hire you?"

This raises an obvious question: how would you know about the inner workings of a company you don't even work for? As with any successful marketing, it takes some research.

You can get a general knowledge of prospective employers by keeping abreast of business news, and get more specific information from your local library and the Internet. But personal contacts are the most valuable resource.

Mark S. Granovetter, a Harvard University sociologist and author of *Getting a Job: A Study of Contacts and Careers,* investigated how people get professional, technical and managerial jobs. He found that only 10 percent get their jobs through ads, 9 percent find them through agencies, and the majority — 74 percent — find their jobs through some type of personal contact.

"Personal contacts are of paramount importance in connecting people with jobs," says Granovetter. "Better jobs are found through contacts, and the best jobs, the ones with the highest pay and prestige and affording the greatest satisfaction to those in them, are most apt to be filled in this way." He also found that about 44 percent of the jobs obtained this way were new positions created for the applicant.

It may seem that you simply don't know too many people — perhaps no one — who could possibly be a contact that leads to a job you want. That may be true, if you limit "personal contacts" to your current friends and acquaintances, which means it's time to create some new contacts.

An acquaintance of mine had a job-hunting experience that illustrates the point. After moving across the country because her husband's business demanded relocation, she started answering want ads and sending out resumes — lots of them. With an MBA and about ten years of impressive experience, she was completely unprepared for the response. Most companies didn't even acknowledge receipt of her resume.

After months of frustration, she looked up a former classmate from her MBA program, who introduced her to a local chapter of a professional organization. With time on her hands, she volunteered to help organize an upcoming conference and

making your plan

You can use this checklist as a guide.

Skills you currently use _____

_____

Skills you don't use _____

_____

Possible increase in compensation_____

Skills you need most to increase your market value

_____

_____

Which of these could increase your market value the most?

_____

Immediate priority (circle one)   marketing   learning new skills

Marketing To-Do List	Learning To-Do List
_____	_____
_____	_____
_____	_____
_____	_____
_____	_____

ended up being one of the key people who made the event a success. In the process, she learned about a very appealing job opening, applied, had numerous interviews over a period of several months and got the job — where she's worked happily for the last ten years. How much time elapsed between her contacting the classmate and getting the job? Nearly a year.

Since I am continually looking for a new job, in the sense of being another new client's financial planner, I can also validate the personal-contact theory. Besides, my clients don't run want ads to find me.

Keep in mind, though, that people do get jobs through want ads and agencies. Another acquaintance of mine has been moving rapidly up the management ranks in the publishing industry and every one of her jobs has come from a want ad, in a local newspaper, industry magazine or on the Internet — an information source that is bringing a new dimension to the hiring process.

The Internet makes it possible for you to post your resume for employers to find, as well as apply for specific advertised positions. (If you're concerned about your current employer finding out you're looking for a new job, some career Web sites enable you to screen who sees your resume.) The resume-posting feature is a bit like listing your business in the Yellow Pages, something job applicants could never do in the past.

One last word about marketing: you may have skills you've never had a chance to use in the workaday world, so an employer is reticent to give you fair credit. For example, you may be extremely good at managing projects but have never had the opportunity to demonstrate this talent at work. Demonstrating your competence is critical, and you may be able to get that experience by doing some volunteer work where you manage a challenging project, then show the results.

All in all, marketing yourself demands some creativity, but it's a very worthwhile investment.

resources

Toastmasters World Headquarters www.toastmasters.org
UCLA Continuing Education Online www.uclaextension.org

College Degrees Online www.phoenix.edu

The University of Phoenix has been offering online degree programs for working professionals since 1989. The curriculum requires 15 to 20 hours per week and above-average self-discipline, according to the university.

Career Web Sites

The following Web sites contain a wealth of career-planning information, including links to sites where you can do your research about prospective employers. They offer job listings, which can be searched by area and type of job, and databases where you can post a resume online. Some also offer samples of good resumes and letters, how-to information, self-assessments to help you pinpoint goals, questionnaires and checklists to help plan your career, online discussions with experts, information about specific industries and organizations, business trends, and links to Web sites specializing in different fields. Some sites enable you to define the job you are looking for and will notify you by email when new job postings match your criteria.

America's Learning Exchange www.alx.org

CareerBuilder www.careerbuilder.com

JobOptions www.joboptions.com

Monster Board www.monster.com

CareerSite www.careersite.com

Career City www.careercity.com

Ask The Headhunter www.asktheheadhunter.com

chapter 4

Spending Wisely

E arning a good income is certainly one ingredient of financial success, but how much we earn doesn't necessarily
determine our financial destiny. During the past decade,
Americans overall have increased their earnings, but spending
has risen even faster, while personal savings have declined.

In 1997, the Commerce Department reported that the savings rate fell to 2.1 percent, the lowest since the Great
Depression. In July of that year, consumer spending rose 0.8
percent, while personal income after taxes rose by only 0.1 percent. And *American Demographics* reports that 60 percent of the
nation has enough financial assets to maintain their current
lifestyle for only one month — a precarious way to live.

You might blame rising costs. After all, a lot of years have
passed since a cup of coffee cost ten cents. But a Federal
Reserve Bank study in 1998 found that the real cost of living in
this country has fallen dramatically since the 1950s, when a typical home sold for $14,500. Back then it took an average of 6.5
hours of work to pay for one square foot of that home. In the
late 1990s, when that home cost $140,000, it took only 5.6 hours
of work to pay for a square foot.

Overall, basic living expenses today devour a significantly
smaller percentage of paychecks than they used to. Compare
these averages: the 1950 family spent 54.8 percent of its income
on food, shelter and clothes, whereas today's family spends only
37.7 percent. So where does all the extra money go?

Disappearing Dollars

A local television news teams ran an interesting experiment: Two people went to the same supermarket with identical shopping lists. One looked for the best price on each item and rang up a bill of about $60, while the other didn't pay attention to price at all and spent a whopping $150. The price-savvy shopper spent an extra 20 minutes to save $90 — a very good return for a little extra time.

Your food shopping basket may not have such obvious savings potential, but chances are, some of your hard-earned cash is disappearing in ways that are difficult to account for, and if you can identify some of these, it may be easier to save money than you think. These are some experiments you can try for yourself:

- Pretend you're about to move to a remote location, so remote that the cost of moving your possessions is astronomical — half the cost of what you originally paid for each item. Go through a room in your home, including closets or cupboards, and decide what to pack.
- Pick a closet, cupboard or storage area that has a lot of "stuff" in it. List each thing you've used less than ten times in the past year. Write down what you paid for it, then add the total for the list.
- Imagine you could convert some of your possessions to cash — the actual price you paid for them. Make a list of what you would sell, the dollar value of each and the total.

If you have no extraneous possessions, recognize that you're in a minority, but before you give yourself a pat on the back, ask yourself if there are any services you pay for that are of little or no value to you. Do you subscribe to magazines you never read, or online services you don't use? Do you pay for premium cable channels you don't need? Is there a discount travel serv-

the bigger picture

Money has a way of getting spent, either in places you planned or elsewhere. Day by day, as we make choices to purchase things, it's easy to take a short-term view. But a look at the bigger picture can offer some motivation to be more discriminating about how you spend your cash.

Is it realistic to think that you could save one out of every $100 you earn? What about two, or five, or ten? How worthwhile could it be?

As an example, if you saved $1,000 per year ($83.33 per month or $19.23 per week) and earned 10 percent annually, excluding any tax considerations, you would have:

	Dollars saved	Dollars accumulated
In 5 years:	5,000	6,716
In 10 years:	10,000	17,531
In 15 years:	15,000	34,950
In 20 years:	20,000	63,002
In 25 years:	25,000	108,182
In 30 years:	30,000	180,943
In 35 years:	35,000	298,127

ice you subscribed to through one of your credit cards, but never use? I've met people who have had monthly payments deducted from their checking accounts for an insurance policy they had no records for. They remembered buying something but had no idea of what exactly or from which company.

The Dreaded "B" Word

There are people who are shopaholics — compulsive shoppers. Sometimes they make interesting guests on daytime talk shows. But true compulsive shoppers, dramatic as their stories can be, are few in numbers. However, people who continually exercise forethought when spending money are also rare, as are their financial accomplishments. One of their secrets for success is a very old, tried and tested concept that seems to have fallen out of favor: a budget.

I call it "the dreaded B word" because so many people have looked at me, aghast, when I've simply mentioned the word in financial consultations. Reactions vary from, "But I work hard and I deserve to enjoy myself," to an amused, "You've got to be kidding." For whatever reason, the word conjures up images of self-deprivation, a stoic life with little joy.

In practice, having some realistic financial goals and actively working toward them can add a whole new and pleasant dimension to day-to-day living. Imagine going on a vacation but having no idea where you're headed or what you will do. If you get tired of waiting at a traffic light, you just turn a corner and drive down a side street. So what if it's a dead end; you're not trying to get anywhere in particular. Maybe that's your idea of fun. And if you end up hungry, tired and out of gas late at night in a bad neighborhood? You get the idea.

Imagine another scenario: You get a promotion and a raise in salary. The first thing you do is lease a new car, one which you couldn't afford before. Now, driving to work is a real pleasure. You finally take that vacation that was always out of reach, and you just manage to qualify for a mortgage for the bigger home your friends admire so much. Why worry about a financial cushion? You're on top of the world — until your employer merges with a bigger company and lays off a few hundred people, including you. It happens.

In today's culture, you don't have to be a shopaholic to spend your earnings very quickly. If you watch network television, about 25 percent of your programming — advertising — is produced solely to make you buy things. In magazines, the percentage of advertising can be much higher.

Think of it this way: some of the world's most brilliant marketing minds are doing their best to induce you to want everything from $100 running shoes to a new car, and even the latest prescription drug. Whether or not you need any of these things, or whether you truly want them, is beside the point. Marketing exists to make the product desirable in your mind, and it's very effective.

So am I suggesting that you deprive yourself of all these things — maybe even get rid of your TV and never look at another magazine? That would be like going on a fad diet to lose some unbelievable amount of weight in a week. Those diets don't work, and neither would such a "budgeting" approach. What does work is a realistic approach: Plan your spending before the money leaves your hands. Make sure the plan is one you can follow and that it's in line with your personal goals. Easier said than done, you might well think.

Making a Spending Plan

The first step in making a useful spending plan — a budget without the dread — is to know where all your money is going. If you can account for every penny and have it written down somewhere already, pull it out for reference. Otherwise, pull out whatever records you have and start making a list of everything you have spent money on, preferably in the past twelve months. You need to see that much history; otherwise, you won't account for annual expenses, like your car registration, for example, or gifts during holidays; and leaving those out can seriously trip you up later. You can try the format on the next page or use the more detailed worksheet in the Appendix.

Getting Control

Once you see accurately where your money has been going, you'll have to set some priorities if you want to accumulate some savings (aka wealth). You might be thinking, "But you said

spending worksheet

Month _____

Recurring monthly expenses:
(Include credit card or other debt payments made — the actual amount paid that month.)

Expense   Amount

_____   _____

_____   _____

_____   _____

_____   _____

_____   _____

_____   _____

_____   _____

_____   _____

_____   _____

                           Subtotal: _____

Other expenses that month:

Expense   Amount

_____   _____

_____   _____

_____   _____

_____   _____

_____   _____

_____   _____

_____   _____

_____   _____

                           Subtotal: _____

                              Total: _____

          Total income for that month: _____

          Subtract total expenses above: _____

                         Difference: _____

If the difference between your total income and expenses didn't come close to zero, recall as best you can what created the difference. This is very important because whatever those hidden expenses are could be a major reason why money always seems to disappear too fast.

this isn't a process of self-deprivation." It isn't, unless you consider deprivation to be anything but spending every cent (and more) with abandon.

Smart spending comes down to getting good value for your money, which most of us want. In practice, it means consciously planning and spending to get good value. For example, a car that turns out to be a lemon, no matter how low the cost, isn't worth much. But if you buy a car you can't really afford and live with the resulting stress, and pass up opportunities to earn substantial money (see The Bigger Picture chart earlier in this chapter), that's not such a good deal either. Or, if you spend a bundle on a great meal you can't afford, the aftertaste may not be what the chef intended.

The biggest hurdle in this process is to make a plan that realistically furthers your own goals. If you feel you're accomplishing something important by spending — or not spending — it's quite likely that you'll follow the roadmap you create.

The Planning Process

Your financial goals can be long- or short-term at this point in the process. They may be as obvious as getting out of debt or buying a home or saving for your children's college education or building a retirement nest egg. Whatever the goal or goals, writing them down is critical, and this is the time to do it. Then, take your list of the previous year's expenses and take the following steps:

■ **Rate each expense for value, on a scale of one to ten**
The top score means that expense has very high value to you, enough that you would forego other things in order to have whatever that money is buying. Here's where personal priorities really enter the picture and why this isn't an exercise in self-deprivation: You plan to spend on that which is really important

to you. Let's say you know you could spend $3,000 less per year on a car. If that car is definitely more valuable to you than having about $20,000 in cash five years from now, or about $50,000 ten years from now (see The Bigger Picture), then you are getting very good value. If you rate the value of that car as a four or five and would much rather have the cash down the road . . . you decide.

■ Sift the wheat from the chaff

Take the expenses with the lowest scores — you decide what the cut-off point is — and add up their total.

■ Consider your options

Take that total and see what else that money could be used for. Consider all the options that interest you. For example, you could buy something else instead, pay off debt, invest in some type of security (stocks, bonds, mutual funds, etc.), buy real estate, pay off your mortgage, save up for a bigger purchase, use it for a vacation, send your kids to a private school or save for their college education, get more education yourself, start or buy a business, buy art and hang it on your wall, leave the money in a savings account as emergency funds . . . the options are limited only by your own interests, imagination and ability or inability to plan.

■ Set your priorities

If the dollar value of your "chaff" is nonexistent or seems too small to make a difference, you may be living beyond your means, a problem that may require major changes to solve, whether it means increasing your income — if that's practical short-term — or adjusting your lifestyle to match your income as is. But regardless of how much your low-value expenses total, you still need to set priorities.

■ **Draft your spending plan, aka budget**

You may decide to cut some expenses immediately, while others may need to be phased out gradually if you have commitments to meet. For example, if you have a cellular phone you never use but have a legally binding contract with the service provider that runs another two months, paying for the remaining two months, then canceling, may be the best option. Or, you may change your plans about future spending, such as deciding not to buy a new car after all but putting more money in your employer's 401k plan.

The Bottom Line

If it's going to work, your spending plan has to be one you can realistically follow, and it has to include all your expenses. Items that occur less frequently than once a month — quarterly insurance premiums, annual fees, etc., — need to be broken down and planned for before they become due. If not, they will trip you up, and such expenses are one of the reasons people get into trouble with debt . . . but that's a whole other chapter.

resources

Federal Consumer Information Center www.pueblo.gsa.gov

A central source of information about federal programs and consumer information, including many money-saving tips.

Consumer Action www.consumer-action.org

This not-for-profit consumer education and advocacy group offers lots of helpful information about consumer spending, including pitfalls to avoid and ways to save.

chapter 5

Use and Abuse of Debt

P eople have been borrowing money almost as long as history has been recorded, but in recent years, the sheer volume of personal debt in America has been growing to unprecedented levels. Banks have issued credit card lines totaling approximately $10,000 for every man, woman and child, and about one-quarter of that amount is actually owed by card holders. Those numbers don't include mortgages, car loans or any other consumer debt that isn't a revolving line, such as one-time store loans for purchases of computers, furniture and other household goods.

Why do we borrow so much? Not even the major credit card companies know the exact motivation, but there is certainly a visible trend toward more luxury purchases, especially among people who could not find a way to buy such things in earlier years. For example, Simmons Market Research found that in 1998, fur-coat ownership increased by 98 percent in households earning between $20,000 and $30,000. In contrast, households with incomes over $40,000 didn't buy significantly more furs during the same time period.

Robert H. Frank, a Cornell University economics professor, calls this trend "Luxury Fever," also the name of his latest book. Frank contends that middle income Americans are caught in an obsession for luxury purchases, not because of their own stupidity or greed, but because the pursuit of luxury has, in essence, become a fact of life. He points out that since the 1950s, the average American home has doubled in size; the average price of a car (over $22,000) has increased by more than 75 percent in a decade; and spending on luxury items is increasing much more rapidly than overall retail sales. In a typical year during the 1990s, sales of luxury goods rose 21 percent, while sales of merchandise overall rose only 5 percent.

Aside from the desire for luxury, there is another critical factor at work in the credit world: marketing. The credit card industry works very hard to entice you to borrow, more than tripling the number of credit card offers mailed out to consumers during the past decade and increasing the amount of credit issued proportionally. The dollar value of credit extended has grown much more rapidly than consumers' use of it.

We haven't always lived this way. Before 1968, consumers typically borrowed to buy homes, cars and other hard goods that usually served as collateral for the loans, which had a limited term. Enter credit cards and revolving debt started to grow, slowly at first, then gaining momentum. And it just keeps growing and growing. These figures are from the Federal Reserve:

Revolving credit, in millions of dollars	
1968	1,316.77
1978	36,924.59
1988	164,681.90
1998	531,278.12
2002	693,594.46

The Most Deadly Question

The easiest way to accumulate too much debt is to keep asking yourself the most deadly question: Can I afford the minimum payments? According to the Consumer Federation of America, the lowering of minimum payments for credit card debt, from 4 percent to 2-3 percent, has been responsible for much of the rise in consumer bankruptcies during the past decade. The low minimum payment, which barely covers interest, convinces many people that they can afford debt when they can't.

If you want to buy something using credit, a more practical set of questions would be:

- How much will this really cost me?
- How long will I be making payments if I pay only the minimum?
- Can I pay off the debt more quickly, and how much will I be paying in that scenario?
- Is there a really good reason why I have to buy this now, rather than wait until I've saved the money to pay cash?
- Do I really need to buy this at all?

How Long and How Much Will You Pay?

Credit card minimum payments are typically between 2 and 3 percent of the outstanding balance, or a specified minimum (as low as $10 or $20), whichever is higher. If you pay only the minimum and don't charge anything else, the cost of credit can be sky high.

Although the most deadly question is relevant to any type of credit, it is particularly vicious when it comes to credit cards for several reasons: They are the most plentiful type of credit, even among college students who don't have a job and would never dream of applying for a mortgage to buy a home, or even a car loan. The minimum payments on credit card balances will almost never force you to pay off the loan. And the open credit line encourages spending before a balance is paid in full — the perfect foundation for infinite interest payments.

When looking at the chart at right, you may wonder why I've included an interest rate as high as 24 percent. One of the latest developments in credit card charges has been higher interest rates for customers whose payments are late or whose balance exceeds their limit, and these "penalty" interest rates can go as high as 24 percent. A card issuer's right to do this is covered in the fine print, either in the original contract or in amendments that are periodically sent out with bills. Needless to say, if you don't pay attention to those pesky notices, you could be in for a very unpleasant surprise.

With so much debt outstanding, how are American consumers reacting? The Consumer Federation of America has periodically commissioned surveys, asking: "Overall, how concerned would you say you currently are about meeting your credit card monthly payments?" During the past few years, roughly one-third of American adults have been very concerned about being able to pay their credit card bills every month. It's unlikely that anyone would make a conscious choice to live that way.

Is There Ever a Good Reason to Borrow?

Assuming you have a limited supply of funds, yes, borrowing may be a good move. Owning a home and paying off a mortgage rather than paying rent has definite benefits. Unlike rent, mortgage interest is probably tax deductible, and home ownership builds equity. And occasionally, extending a loan longer than you have to can work in your favor. A study at Appalachian State University in Boone, NC, illustrates one of those rare situations.

Professors at Appalachian State compared the benefit of a $150,000 home mortgage amortized over 15 and 30 years. They made the following assumptions: Each homeowner spent the same amount each month for 30 years, including mortgage payments, property taxes, all other home ownership costs, and con-

the real cost of credit card debt

An initial balance of $1,000 at 18% interest could take nearly 13 years to pay off, with more than $1,000 in interest.

A balance of $5,000 at 18% could take over 25 years to pay, with over $7,000 in interest.

If you pay a fixed amount each month, here are a few possible scenarios:

Initial balance: $1,000   Interest rate: 24% annually

Length of loan	1 year	2 years	3 years	4 years	5 years
Monthly payment	95	53	39	33	29
Total interest paid	135	269	412	565	726

Initial balance: $1,000   Interest rate: 18% annually

Length of loan	1 year	2 years	3 years	4 years	5 years
Monthly payment	92	50	36	29	25
Total interest paid	100	198	301	410	524

Initial balance: $1,000   Interest rate: 11% annually

Length of loan	1 year	2 years	3 years	4 years	5 years
Monthly payment	88	47	33	26	22
Total interest paid	61	119	179	241	305

Initial balance: $1,000   Interest rate: 8% annually

Length of loan	1 year	2 years	3 years	4 years	5 years
Monthly payment	87	45	31	24	20
Total interest paid	44	85	128	172	217

Compare the cost of credit above to what your money can earn, page 45.

tributions to a tax-deferred retirement savings plan. Both were in a 33-percent tax bracket, including state and federal taxes. Both lived in their home for 30 years.

Here's how the two scenarios differed: The 15-year-mort-gage holder had higher payments for the first 15 years. During those years, he paid only his mortgage. Starting in year 16, when the mortgage was paid in full, he paid the same amount into his retirement plan. The 30-year-mortgage holder, whose mortgage payments were lower but lasted 30 years, paid the difference into his retirement plan for the full 30 years. Both retirement plans were invested with a 10-percent annual return.

Even though both individuals spent the same amount of money per month for 30 years, their retirement assets, apart from their homes, were quite different. The 30-year mortgage holder had $1.17 million in a retirement nest egg, while the 15-year mortgage holder accumulated only $791,000.

In reality, most home buyers do choose a 30-year mortgage. However, few invest monthly in a tax-deferred retirement plan during those years, and many refinance their homes to cover other debt or expenses – a strategy with its own pitfalls.

Using or Abusing Home Equity

For some people, owning their home free and clear is a major financial goal, one that symbolizes a certain amount of security and financial freedom. If you feel this way, it's best to do every-thing you can to reach that goal. But in today's world, home equity loans are marketed just as vigorously as credit cards, and the pitfalls are just as dangerous.

The most aggressive advertising preys on people's desire for an instant solution to financial pressure: A home equity loan will reduce your monthly payments by consolidating other debt, according to the pitch, and you'll have lots of money left over every month. In practice, using home equity to solve debt prob-lems often leads to worse situations. Most people who overuse credit cards, then pay off balances with home equity loans, end up overspending with their credit cards again, and are left without any equity and in more debt. A real solution to too much debt has to include changing spending habits.

Another pitfall to consider: If you are likely to buy a new home in a few years, more equity in your home puts you in a much better position, because you will have a bigger down payment.

In all fairness, home equity loans do have their place, especially since the interest paid may be tax deductible (don't assume it will be — check with your tax advisor). Home improvements that add value to your home can be a very good investment and a good reason to cash out some of your equity. In some instances, a home equity loan may offer advantages over a car loan, because the interest rate may be much lower and the interest may be tax deductible. However, if the home equity lender charges extra fees, those may outweigh the advantages.

Car Leasing and Buying Options

Leasing has become a common way to finance a car because the monthly payments are lower than those for a loan on a comparable car. In theory, this means the monthly savings could be invested and earn interest — which could be a wise strategy. However, many people lease cars simply because they want to drive something they can't afford to buy. If that is the motivation, leasing probably isn't a good financial choice. But is anyone trying to be rational?

As long as cars have existed, they have been used for more than mere transportation, as symbols of status, youth, sexual prowess, rebellion, financial success and excess. So it isn't surprising that many cars on today's roads are driven by people whose annual incomes are lower than the purchase price of their car.

If you want to buck the trend for the sake of a little extra wealth and peace of mind, these are some key issues to consider:

- The longer you keep a car, the lower your overall cost.
- Paying cash or getting a loan to buy a car will always cost less than leasing in the longer term.
- If you save money by leasing (rather than overextending yourself to drive a car that is beyond your means) and invest those savings, you could be further ahead, but only if you have the discipline to follow through.
- If you have a choice between paying cash or taking out a loan, the only way you will profit from the loan is by investing the cash and earning a higher rate of return than the loan interest rate.

Getting the Best Deal

Regardless of the type of credit, your credit history makes all the difference in obtaining higher or lower interest rates. How you look on paper may or may not seem fair, but it's important to understand how today's system works.

Credit bureaus have been around for a long time, but technology and the volume of credit transactions have led to a very impersonal form of number crunching to rate individual credit worthiness: the FICO score. (The acronym stands for Fair, Isaac & Company, which invented the scoring system.) A formula is used to calculate a number based on over 30 factors. Each credit bureau uses a slightly different formula, so each one produces a slightly different score, but they're all pretty close. The mortgage industry relies most heavily on these numbers, but other lenders use them too. If you've ever applied for a loan or credit card and received a letter of rejection, the reasons given were one or more on the list of criteria used in calculating FICO scores:

- amount owed on accounts is too high
- delinquency on accounts

- too few bank revolving accounts
- too many bank or national revolving accounts
- too many accounts with balances
- consumer finance accounts
- account payment history too new to rate
- too many recent inquiries in the last 12 months
- too many accounts opened in the last 12 months
- proportion of balances to credit limits is too high on revolving accounts
- amount owed on revolving accounts is too high
- length of revolving credit history is too short
- time since delinquency is too recent or unknown
- length of credit history is too short
- lack of recent bank revolving information
- lack of recent revolving account information
- no recent non-mortgage balance information
- number of accounts with delinquency
- too few accounts currently paid as agreed
- time since derogatory public record or collection
- amount past due on accounts
- serious delinquency, derogatory public record, or collection
- too many bank or national revolving accounts with balances
- no recent revolving balances
- proportion of loan balances to loan amounts too high
- lack of recent installment loan information
- date of last inquiry too recent
- time since most recent account opening too short
- number of revolving accounts
- number of bank revolving or other revolving accounts
- number of established accounts
- no recent bankcard balances
- too few accounts with recent payment information.

If you get a copy of your credit report, you may also see your FICO score. Online at www.myfico.com, you can purchase your FICO score and gain access to other information lenders use to asses your credit worthiness. The system is complex, but there are a few rules of thumb for improving your score and your ability to get better rates:

- Always pay your bills on time.
- Check your credit report with each of the credit bureaus periodically and get any errors corrected. Credit bureaus are becoming more consumer friendly, with toll-free lines to answer questions and reports that are understandable.
- Don't use credit lines to the limit; keep your debt under 75 percent of the credit available.
- Avoid too many credit inquiries, as these can signal that you're in financial trouble or likely to overextend yourself.

Digging Out of Trouble

Whether you're in over your head, want to pay off debt more quickly, or just want to get smarter about using credit, there are plenty of free resources to help, through education and counseling. The oldest among these, Consumer Credit Counseling Services (CCCS), is a nonprofit agency with offices around the country that can be found in your local phone book. Other organizations provide similar services, but CCCS has a much stronger emphasis on education and, unlike some other groups, doesn't charge for many seminars covering just about every aspect of credit wisdom.

Credit counseling at CCCS can result in a payment plan you execute yourself, meeting and exceeding the minimum payments of all your creditors. Or, if that's impossible, the agency offers a debt management plan. Then, it works with each of your creditors to establish lower payments that you can meet;

you pay one monthly sum to CCCS, and it pays your creditors. You also pay a small monthly fee for the service.

CCCS and similar organizations have ongoing relationships with creditors and receive financial support from some of them, so they can negotiate more effectively than an individual consumer. Creditors' concessions can include decreasing interest and finance charges, or "reaging" credit cards, which works like resetting a clock. Let's say you are two payments past due; if the card is reaged, after your next payment or two, the card will be considered current without your having to pay the extra past due amount.

Debt management plans have helped people get out of overwhelming debt in three to five years. However, there is a downside: your credit rating does suffer. Once your debts are paid, CCCS can work with you to reestablish good credit, but that does take time — years. Although a debt management plan is not as black a mark as bankruptcy, it isn't something that should be entered into lightly.

Not surprisingly, the business of credit counseling has mushroomed, with its own pitfalls. Some organizations focus on debt management plans and may steer you into one unnecessarily. Others offer a lot of educational material for a fee, so you could end up spending several hundred dollars you can ill afford.

In addition there is another type of business, "credit repair," which is in no way affiliated with credit counseling but claims to magically repair bad credit reports, usually for hefty upfront fees. It sounds, and is, too good to be true. Legally, a creditor is not obliged to remove negative information from your credit report if it's true. Credit repair companies claim to have special secret methods, which usually involve flooding creditors with letters demanding documentation to support reports of late payments, in the hopes that creditors will buckle under the sheer volume of paperwork and remove negative, though accurate, information.

The bottom line is, there's no magic bullet. Negative credit information remains on credit bureau reports for seven years, except for bankruptcies, which remain for ten years.

Grabbing the Reins

Whether you use or abuse credit depends primarily on your perspective. If you realistically estimate the consequences of borrowing before taking the plunge, chances are, credit will work in your favor. For example, you could use cash as a down payment on a home and borrow to buy a car. If the payments are within your comfort zone, you should be further ahead than if your were to rent a home and pay cash for the car.

When deciding whether or not to use credit, consider the following:

- Your monthly debt payments, aside from a mortgage, should not exceed 20 percent of your after-tax income. In the case of credit cards, include a sufficient monthly payment to pay off the balance in a reasonable period of time.
- To avoid having to use credit in emergencies, you should have between three and six months of living expenses set aside.
- When considering a loan or credit card purchase, calculate how many hours or days you will have to work to pay off the principal, and how much additional labor will be required to pay the interest. Then decide whether it's worth it.

Above all, know where you stand. If you have outstanding debt, keep a current list of its status. Use the Debt Worksheet in this chapter or develop your own format, but stay on top of it. With an accurate picture, you can use credit as you choose, rather than letting it use you.

debt worksheet

Creditor	Amount owed	Annual interest rate	Monthly payment	Monthly finance charge	Principal paid	Approximate date when monthly balance will be paid in full

There are other basic concepts I haven't belabored, such as using credit cards with the lowest interest rate available or paying off the ones with the highest rates first. I believe that, as a rational individual, you would naturally do such things — if you decide to be in control. And, if you haven't already done so, I hope you do make that decision.

resources

Bankrate.com www.bankrate.com

The site will help you to calculate the cost of your personal debt and how to pay it off more quickly, and help you obtain current information about the best terms available for mortgages, home equity loans, auto loans, ATM and credit cards, and all types of bank accounts.

Auto Lease Guide www.leaseguide.com

Extensive information about leasing cars, including calculators to compare buying and leasing the car of your choice.

National Foundation for Credit Counseling www.nfcc.org

Information about credit bureaus, credit reports, education and credit counseling services throughout the United States.

chapter 6

Income Tax –
Avoiding the Traps

I've never had a client tell me: "I'd like to give the IRS a little extra money." Yet most tax filers do just that, and they're very happy about their contribution. In fact, the "extra" is not so little, totaling more than $100 billion annually. What am I talking about? Tax refunds. They seem to be increasing every year, averaging close to $2,000.

If you look forward to your annual refund, you probably don't agree with my logic. After all, you get a nice little windfall every year, so what could be wrong with that? Nothing, if you don't mind depriving yourself of more than a little wealth. The tax refund is the most popular tax trap of all, but it stems from the same source as all the others: lack of tax planning.

Timing Is Everything

Early each year, before the memories of New Year's resolutions have faded, "tax season" starts rearing its head. We are inundated with tax tips through every available media channel, and professionals who prepare tax returns resign themselves to marathon schedules. Unfortunately, most of this hectic activity is taking place at least a year too late. You needed the tax advice at the beginning of the previous year, so that you could act on the information to minimize your tax bill.

In practice, most people get tax advice only when their return needs to be prepared. It's a bit like going on a badly planned fishing trip, and although the analogy may seem far-fetched, it isn't.

Let's say you know fishing is very good in a certain lake, which is situated way out in the wilderness. It's a two-day hike to get there so you only bring the food you think you'll need, expecting to eat the fish you catch. When you arrive, you discover a lake so polluted that the fish is inedible — you don't have enough food. Luckily, you find a local wilderness expert who shows you which berries are safe to eat, so that you have the energy to hike back to civilization.

The tax preparer is a last-minute wilderness guide? Odd as it may seem, when you seek tax advice solely when it's time to prepare your return, that's what you're asking that professional to be. Whether your tax advisor is a CPA or an Enrolled Agent (tax professionals who are certified by the federal government to represent taxpayers before the IRS), that individual is very well qualified to prepare your return. However, chances are, your relationship with them doesn't go as far as tax planning year-round. Yet planning — determining what will work best in your personal situation — is the process that can reduce your tax bill and make your piggy bank gain some weight.

Simple Saving Strategies

I don't need to tell you that taxes are a complex subject, and proper planning requires some effort. Even if you rely on a professional advisor, you will benefit most from that relationship by having an understanding of the basics. But before I address those, remember a couple of key points:

■ If you received a refund last year, adjust the amount of tax that is withheld from your paycheck. Use the money to accumulate some wealth for yourself rather than giving the IRS an interest-free loan.

- Whether you received a refund or not, invest as much as possible in any tax-deferred retirement vehicle that is available to you, such as your employer's 401k plan or an IRA. (These types of plans are discussed in Chapter 10.)

a plan in time . . .

Nearly half of all taxpayers don't know whether they have overpaid or underpaid their taxes until they prepare their tax return, according to a survey by Minneapolis-based Lutheran Brotherhood. That's a pretty precarious position to be in, but it is largely avoidable, if you have a sense of the basic principles that underlie all tax planning.

What you need to know	Projected numbers needed
1. Your income for the coming year	
From a tax perspective, there are two main categories of income: earned, or what you get paid for the work you do, and capital gains, or profits you receive from the sale of stocks, bonds, mutual fund shares, real estate or other assets. Each is taxed differently, and how much you receive in the "earned" category affects your tax rate on capital gains. Interest and dividends from assets you own are treated somewhat differently, but the tax rate on these is also influenced by your earned income.	■ Total earned income (wages, tips, commissions, self-employment income) ■ Capital gains or losses from the sale of any asset outside a tax-deferred retirement plan ■ All interest and dividend income outside a tax-deferred retirement plan
2. Your projected deductions	
Some of the key categories of deductions include (but do not apply in all situations): tax-deductible retirement plans, dependents, mortgage interest and other home ownership costs (described in more detail below), expenses incurred as an employee, charitable donations, home equity interest, student loan interest, education costs, child care, alimony payments, investment expenses, and business expenses for the self-employed.	■ Every deductible, or potentially deductible expense, listed by category; include tax-deductible contributions to 401ks, IRAs or other qualified retirement plans

continued on next page

a plan in time . . . continued

What you need to know	Projected numbers needed
3. Any tax credits you qualify for	
Unlike deductions, which are subtracted from your taxable income, tax credits are subtracted from the amount of actual tax you owe, e.g., a $500 tax credit means your tax bill is $500 less.	■ Dollar value of any tax credits you will be eligible for
4. An estimate of the taxes you will owe	
The previous year's tax return may be a useful guide, but the calculations will need to be adjusted for the coming year, especially if you are expecting a major change, in business or in your personal life, that may impact your tax status.	■ Taxes that will be withheld by an employer ■ Estimated taxes on any self-employment income ■ Estimated taxes on projected capital gains, interest and dividend income
5. Possible events with tax consequences	
Although it isn't possible to predict life across the boards, we often have some idea of impending major events, whether personal or work-related. Changes that affect our tax status may include marriage, divorce, child birth, starting a part- or full-time business, a higher commission level or employee bonus, buying or selling a home or other property, and buying or selling investments.	■ Dollar amounts for bonuses, changes in commissions or tips, selling price of assets to be sold and original purchase price and any related costs

If you like crunching numbers and delving through tax-related information, there is a lot you can do yourself, especially if you also like computers and use tax-preparation software. On the other hand, if the idea of compiling the above list seems completely overwhelming, get some professional help at the outset.

In looking for an advisor, the most important thing is to find someone who specializes in planning. I can't emphasize that enough, because I've seen too many instances of missed opportunities to reduce taxes when planning has not been the main thrust of an advisor's services. Even if you opt for the do-it-yourself approach, I recommend getting your strategy and calculations checked by a qualified professional. If you do your homework well, professional advice will be but a small investment, because it won't take a lot of time for a competent advisor to review your estimates. And, if you do educate yourself, any questions you may have won't take long to answer.

Regardless of which approach you choose, the most important step is to take action at or before the start of the year. Daunting as the process may seem, it does get easier with practice, and the benefits are well worth the effort.

Ways to Reduce Your Taxes

Once you see where you stand, you can explore your options. One good way to do this is to look at some "what if" scenarios. For example, if you don't contribute the maximum allowable amount to a 401k or an IRA, see how much you can save in taxes and build in wealth by increasing your contribution. If you're an employee but have always wanted to have your own business, consider starting one part-time with a home office. Or, if you don't own a home, consider how owning, rather than renting, would change your situation.

In order to see how much you can save with any deduction, you need to know your tax rate, which can vary considerably over the next few years, according to the Economic Growth and Tax Reconciliation Act of 2001.

In addition to federal income taxes, you may also be paying state income tax. Each state has its own rules, and you may also be saving on state taxes by investing in a tax-deferred retirement plan. If you own a home, you may be able to deduct the amount you pay in property taxes from your federal income tax bill.

On the down side, the above deductions do not reduce the amount you pay for Social Security and Medicare. These are frequently referred to as FICA taxes, after the law that mandated we pay them, the Federal Insurance Contributions Act. For Social Security tax, you pay 6.2 percent of wages up to a ceiling that rises each year, and your employer pays the same amount. Self-employed people pay the entire 12.4 percent but can deduct half of the tax as a business expense. For Medicare, employees and employers each pay 1.45 percent of total wages. The self-employed pay the full 2.9 percent, but again, the employer portion is a tax-deductible business expense.

Tax-deferred savings are another way to reduce your tax bill, but you may not be terribly excited about such a plan if your tax rate is low. Obviously, if you only pay 15 percent in federal taxes, you don't save as much as the person paying a much higher rate. While that's true, there are two important factors to consider: The IRS imposes ceilings on tax-deductible retirement contributions. And most important, dollars you save for retirement are worth much more than the immediate tax savings. The compounding of your investment without taxes taking a bite, both at the outset and along the way, results in a much bigger nest egg for you.

how taxes impact the growth of savings

$100/month invested for 20 years at 10% annually	Result
Tax-deductible contribution with tax-deferred growth	$75,937
Tax-deductible contribution with investment returns taxed at 15 percent each year	$62,700
Taxes are paid on each $100, the balance is invested, then taxes are deducted each year from investment returns at a 15-percent tax rate	$53,295

These scenarios show what can happen to $100 per month invested for 20 years at 10 percent annual interest, depending on how taxes come into play. These examples consider federal income tax only. State taxes, where applicable, would further decrease returns on taxable investments.

Benefits of tax-deferred investing would be even greater in higher tax brackets. However, even with a 15-percent tax rate, over a 20-year period, tax-deductible, tax-deferred savings can increase the value of your dollar by over 40 percent!

America's Dream Deduction

Of all the tax-saving strategies, the American dream of home ownership is the most prevalent, and its popularity is growing. Tax deductions for homeowners can include:

- mortgage interest on a primary residence and on a second home, on debt up to $1 million
- interest on a home equity loan up to $100,000, but all of it may not be deductible if your total mortgage amount exceeds the value of your home
- property taxes.

In addition, home owners are more likely to be able to claim other deductions, such as:

- state and local taxes paid
- charitable donations
- other miscellaneous expenses, such as job hunting expenses or significant medical costs, if these exceed certain thresholds.

These types of expenses fall in the category of itemized deductions. The IRS gives taxpayers a choice of claiming these as an alternative to standard deductions which everyone is entitled to. The standard deductions are fixed amounts, adjusted each year for inflation.

If you don't own a home, the tax impact of buying one will vary, based on your personal circumstances. If the deductible home ownership expenses, plus any other itemized deductions, add up to more than your standard deduction, you're ahead.

In discussing home ownership, I never recommend buying a home primarily for tax benefits. The monthly cash outlay for ownership is usually significantly higher than renting a comparable residence, when all the upkeep costs are included. However, in addition to potential tax benefits, owning creates the opportunity to live rent-free once your mortgage is paid off. And if you decide to convert your equity to cash by selling, some very attractive tax benefits are available.

If you have lived in your home for two of the previous five years, capital gain from the sale of your home, up to $250,000 for an individual, or $500,000 for a married couple, is not taxable. The capital gain is essentially the difference between your purchase and sale prices. Money spent on capital improvements may add to your purchase price, decreasing the gain when you sell.

However, the tax-free amounts are not as generous as they may seem. Before 1997, gain on the sale of a home was not taxable only if you spent your profits on another home, which most people did. Now, when the capital gains on a home sale are calculated, they take into account untaxed profits from earlier homes that have been invested into your current abode.

Here's an example: Let's say you sold a home ten years ago, made $120,000 profit and reinvested that into your current home. If you're single and profited another $150,000 on a home sale now, you would have a total gain of $270,000. That's $20,000 over the $250,000 tax-free amount. Because that $20,000 is a capital gain, rather than earned income, it would be taxed at one of two capital gains rates.

How Capital Gains Tax Rates Work

This two-tier tax on the taxable portion of profits from the sale of a home also applies to profits from selling other assets, such as stocks, bonds, mutual fund shares, and some other types of property and business assets. However, when selling assets such as securities, the favorable capital gains rate applies only if you have held the investment for twelve months or more. Additional reduction in the rate may kick in if you've owned the property for more than five years.

This is how this tax may work: If you have held the asset for more than five years and your top tax rate is 15 percent, capital gains may be taxed at 8 or 10 percent; if your top tax rate is higher, the capital gains tax may be 18 or 20 percent. If you are close to the limit for the 15 percent federal tax rate and a capital gain puts you into a higher range, the capital gains tax would be prorated. When planning to sell stocks, bonds or mutual fund shares, it's wise to consult a tax professional before making a final decision about when to sell, to make sure tax implications are included in the equation.

Assets are not always sold at a profit. Losses offset gains, but you can only deduct losses that are less than or equal to your capital gains for the year. If the losses are higher than the gains, you may be able to use some or all of the loss amount to offset a portion of your work-related income in a year. In some instances, a portion of the loss may be carried over to future years.

If you receive income from stock dividends or bond interest, keep in mind that this is not a capital gain but income that is taxed at your regular tax rate, just like wages. If you have such taxable investments but don't really need the income, it makes sense to consider reinvesting those assets in growth stocks or mutual funds. That way, if you keep the investments for at least 12 months, you will be taxed at a lower rate. And until you sell, you won't be paying taxes while those assets grow.

Calculating capital gains tax rates today is more complex than ever. Before you count on any of this favorable tax treatment, I always recommend getting competent professional advice because there may be individual circumstances that affect your eligibility.

Home Office Perks and Pitfalls

Another approach that can sometimes save on taxes is setting up a home office and deducting the associated business expenses. These perks are not limited to full-time businesses. If you set up a home office for the convenience of your employer, or if you have a part-time business, your expenses may be deductible, including a percentage of rent, utilities or home ownership costs. However, if you do own your home, those deductions will impact your tax-free capital gains amount when you sell your home, so it's best to evaluate how this will work for you with a professional.

As with home purchases, I never advise anyone to set up a home business for the sake of tax deductions. Self employment, even on a part-time basis, is not for everyone — if you are currently self-employed, I suspect you would agree. A business can be more of an expensive headache than an asset if it exists for the wrong reasons. But if starting your own venture is truly something you want to do, then there are tax advantages available.

Keep a Vigilant Eye on New Developments

Tax laws change from year to year, and if you aren't aware of changes that may save you money, you could definitely miss out. For example, the 1998 tax year saw the introduction of a child tax credit, an adoption credit, and the Lifetime Learning Tax Credit, which offsets the cost of education for you or your children. And changes in 2001 began a series of annual tax-rate adjustments that take effect over a period of several years. All in all, a smart taxpayer requires more knowledge today than at any time in the past to take advantage of all the deductions the law allows.

As with other aspects of your personal finances, the determination to be in the driver's seat is the most critical step. If you simply prepare your tax return (even with the help of a professional), perhaps wait for a refund, and give no further thought to taxes . . . well, let's hope that's not the road you choose.

resources

Internal Revenue Service www.irs.gov

Online publications cover every aspect of income taxes; the site also includes tax forms and information about filing returns electronically.

National Association of Enrolled Agents www.naea.org

The organization provides tax-related information and help in locating an Enrolled Agent in your area.

Quicken www.quicken.com

Although the site sells Quicken's software products, it also offers plenty of useful, free information, including online financial calculators.

chapter 7

Insurance Basics

Unlike many other important purchases, the process of buying insurance isn't usually accompanied by exuberance or excitement. It's not as though you can tell your friends: "Hey, it goes 0 to 60 in . . ." Think of your reaction if you heard someone say: "Wow, I can't believe what a fantastic life insurance policy I heard about today. I can't wait to get my blood drawn so that my application can get processed right away!" Apart from sounding ridiculous, the idea is a bit macabre.

Also unlike other expenditures, insurance is most often purchased with the hope that it will never be used. You don't want to test drive your auto insurer's claims procedure. So, why bother? What you're really buying is peace of mind, both for yourself and for those you care about. Because that peace seems like an intangible, and one that is hard to miss if you've never experienced it, it's very easy to misestimate the need. It's only when the necessity to make a claim arises that the value of your purchase really hits home. Unfortunately, people don't always project their insurance needs realistically.

One survey showed that among those whose spouses had life insurance, 45 percent of widows and 37 percent of widowers said they didn't have enough coverage. Conducted by LIMRA International, Inc., a marketing research organization in the financial services industry, the study found these survivors struggling financially within one to two years after the spouse's death.

No one enjoys thinking about tragedy, but while insurance planning seems to necessitate doing so, one can look at it from a more positive perspective. Insurance, regardless of the type, can alleviate stress from worrying about "what if . . ." And how much is that worth? Although it's impossible to pinpoint a dollar value, less worry and stress can not only make your life more enjoyable, but it can also prevent illness.

Medical research has found definite links between emotional health and all types of physical ailments, from minor ones like colds and flu to debilitating conditions — such as heart disease and cancer — that impact the length and quality of life. To the extent that insurance gives you greater peace of mind, it may help you live a healthier, longer life.

Insurance Planning Pitfalls

Forty or fifty years ago, Americans in all income brackets were much more likely to have an ongoing relationship with an insurance agent in their community. That individual took care of all, or at least many, of their insurance needs over a span of years, tracking changes such as the birth of children, a move-up to a larger home, the purchase of a new car, etc. In the intervening decades, that type of relationship has generally gone the way of the proverbial picket fence.

During the same years, the insurance and financial services industry has evolved into such a complex world that it is difficult for an insurance professional to be able to keep up with all the available products and the regulations governing their sale. And competition for consumers' dollars keeps growing.

The upshot of these developments is that the financial and insurance professionals with the most training and expertise generally focus their attention on the highest income earners — about the top ten to fifteen percent. The rest of America is given plenty of opportunities to buy individual insurance products, but without the benefit of a trained eye to orchestrate all the pieces into a coherent scheme. And more and more, these products are offered through the mail, by telemarketers, or online — with little or no personal contact whatsoever from a trained professional.

There isn't anything wrong with the products themselves — they frequently represent very good value — but there is a danger of buying too much of one, too little of another, and leaving critical gaps in coverage. For example, when a natural disaster strikes, there are always some homeowners who thought they were insured against damage from flood, an earthquake or a hurricane, only to discover, too late, that their homeowners policy excluded such losses.

Reading and understanding insurance contracts can be a tedious process. In fact, I've met plenty of insurance agents who never even attempt to do it. When meeting with prospective clients, they simply present the pitch their company has given them and hope they close the sale. All this is done in good faith, by good people who honestly believe in their product. (Yes, there are some bad apples who knowingly misrepresent the facts, but here, I'm talking about the ones who are trying to do an honest job.)

Fortunately, there is a way to survive in the jungle: arm yourself with knowledge. You don't have to digest an insurance encyclopedia, but you do have to grasp some basics.

The Starting Point

Understanding your own insurance needs lays the foundation for getting the insurance you do need, without wasting money on coverage you don't need. To get a handle on your own situation, the following chart shows some of the questions you should answer to determine which types of insurance you need.

insurance primer

Ask yourself	Type of insurance that applies
If you were unable to work because of an accident or illness, how would you fulfill your financial obligations?	Disability
If you were hospitalized or needed ongoing outpatient medical treatment, how much would your health plan cover and how much would you have to pay out of pocket?	Health
Does your auto insurance provide the right amount of coverage and does it take into account all discounts you may be eligible for?	Auto
Do you know how your homeowners or renters insurance actually works, i.e., would it suffice in a worst-case scenario, and does it cover any natural disasters that may strike your community?	Homeowners or renters
If you have a home office, are your equipment and records adequately insured?	Additions to homeowners or renters
Through business or other activities, are you in a position where you might get sued, incurring personal liability that is not covered by your auto or homeowners or renters policies?	Personal umbrella, auto, homeowners or renters
Is there anyone in your life who would suffer financial hardship if you were to die, and if so, do you have sufficient life insurance to provide for them financially?	Life
Do you have parents, in-laws, other relatives or close friends who you may have to care for as they get older, and if so, how would that care be paid for? Do you know how you (and those close to you) would cope in the later years of your own life if you were not able to take care of yourself 100 percent?	Long term care

Weighing Your Options

Once you have an idea of the type of protection you need, it's helpful to have some sense of the options available in insurance policies. The ones discussed below are intended only as a guide and do not replace individual advice you may need from a qualified advisor for your personal situation.

Disability insurance

If you rely on a paycheck for your income, protecting your ability to work is critical. There are two main ways to do it: through an employer, if this benefit is available, or by purchasing an individual disability policy. The advantage of having your own policy is that it stays with you, if you change jobs, as long as you pay the premiums, so even if you have some coverage through an employer's plan, it may be wise to supplement it on your own.

The range of options in this type of insurance is pretty broad, and picking the wrong ones can be almost as disastrous as having no coverage at all. You really have to sit down with a professional you trust, and that individual must be educated in this subject. However, it helps if you understand a few of the underlying principles:

■ Disability income insurance pays a portion of your salary — up to 60 or 70 percent — if you are unable to work due to disability (unless your disability is job-related, in which case it is covered by workers' compensation insurance, which employers are required to carry by law). There are several reasons why this type of insurance doesn't pay 100 percent: If you pay your premiums with after-tax dollars, your benefits are not taxable. If you are not going to work, insurers assume that your day-to-day expenses will be lower. And, collecting less in disability benefits is viewed as an incentive to return to work as soon as possible.

- Benefits can be payable in two main types of scenarios: if disability prevents you from performing the duties of your normal occupation (sometimes referred to as "own occupation" coverage), or if you are unable to do any type of work at all. If you have specialized skills but don't get the "own occupation" type of insurance, you might never be able to receive benefits, even if you really are disabled from earning a living in your own profession.
- Some policies offer benefits for "residual disability" or "partial disability," prorated based on the percentage of income the disability causes you to lose.
- All policies have a benefit period — a limited amount of time during which benefits are paid.
- All policies spell out a waiting period before benefits kick in.
- Some policies are non-cancelable, meaning the company can't raise your premium, as long as you pay your premiums.
- Most individual policies are guaranteed renewable, meaning the company cannot cancel the policy as long as premiums are paid.

As with any insurance, the more coverage you buy, the more it costs. Your personal needs are the key in all cases, though, and if anyone ever tells you they have a "one size fits all" disability income policy, remember: there's no such thing.

Health insurance

Although a healthy lifestyle is the best insurance of all, even healthy people need to see doctors for checkups. And having a baby, in the best of circumstances, rings up such a sizable bill that many insurance plans either don't cover the event or require a significant extra copayment or deductible. If you're planning to have a family, this is one aspect of your health coverage that you should be very familiar with. Conversely, if you have no possible need for maternity coverage, you might save money with a policy that doesn't provide it. These and other types of decisions about health coverage are becoming more important as, bit by bit, employers are shouldering less of the financial burden.

If your employer offers coverage but expects you to pay a share, you will most likely save money by choosing an HMO option, where you are limited to a specific family doctor and usually must see him or her before seeing any specialist. A plan with more choices will generally cost more, but if those choices are important to you, and affordable . . . it's your decision. If you're self-employed or have no company plan, the healthcare horizon becomes a bit more complex.

In essence, you can use health insurance in two different ways: (a) to minimize your out-of-pocket costs for all healthcare services you expect to use, such as checkups, flu shots and relatively inexpensive medications you may need occasionally, as well as high-cost treatment you hope you will never need; or (b) to cover only the major costs of treating very serious illness or injury, often called "catastrophic" coverage. In situation (b), your premiums will be dramatically lower — half or less — than in (a), but you will pay at least several thousand dollars in deductible and copayment amounts if disaster strikes, and if you need ongoing medication after being discharged from the hospital, it probably won't be covered.

If you have to make a choice between these two types of coverage, realize that the skeleton version in (b) will expose you to quite a bit of financial risk. However, if you can afford only catastrophic coverage, it can still save you from financial ruin if you land in the hospital.

When you reach the age of 65 and become eligible for Medicare, other policies automatically lapse. Because Medicare demands you pay deductibles and copayments, numerous companies offer supplemental, or Medigap, coverage to minimize your costs. If you apply for these within six months of turning 65, the supplemental insurance will cover any health conditions you are already being treated for.

Auto insurance

In 1999, Consumers Union found that auto insurance rates were falling, for the first time since 1974. Two factors were responsible for this trend: safer cars and more mature drivers. At the same time, a survey by the same organization showed that three-quarters of the people who read its magazine, *Consumer Reports,* automatically renewed their auto policies each year without bothering to shop for better rates. Yet when one of the magazine's editors looked online and called insurers directly, she saved almost $800 a year on her own policy. (If you want to know exactly how she did it, check the September 1999 issue of the magazine in a library.)

When it's time to renew your policy, it's also important to see if your circumstances have changed. For example, your rate may drop if you drive less than 7,500 miles a year, or if the teenage driver in your family earned at least a B average or took a qualified driving course. Or, perhaps you should increase the deductible for damage to or theft of your car. You can't save any money if you don't explore your options.

Homeowners or renters insurance

In a national survey conducted by the Insurance Research Council, 60 percent of Americans believe that a natural disaster is likely to strike their community within the next ten years. Yet the majority of these people, whether they owned or rented their home, were not insured against such events, largely because they believed — mistakenly — either that their homeowners policy already provided the protection or that the federal government would offer relief.

In fact, standard homeowners and renters policies do not automatically protect against floods, earthquakes or hurricanes. In some instances, added coverage is available from a private insurer; in others, only government-subsidized plans offer protection. In both cases, you must ask for the coverage. When it comes to the Federal Emergency Management Agency, it is widely misunderstood; most of its relief efforts provide homeowners with low-interest loans, not grants, except where disaster victims have no means to repay a loan.

Disaster coverage is not the only confusing aspect of homeowners and renters insurance. There are two ways policy benefits can work, either in the form of replacement value (paying the present-day cost of replacing what's lost) or actual value (paying only today's market value). Consider your favorite old couch or recliner (let's assume it isn't a priceless antique that is insured accordingly). It's market — or actual — value is negligible, compared with the cost of buying a new one — replacement cost.

In addition, standard homeowners and renters policies place limits on specific types of items, such as jewelry, computers and documents. Find and read these limits and get additional coverage as you need it. If you have a home office, your business assets are most likely underinsured, but you may be able to get either add-on coverage or a separate policy. The key is: if you're paying the premium, make the effort to get a realistic understanding of what is and isn't covered, and for how much.

Personal umbrella policies

If you worry about being the target of lawsuits, a personal umbrella policy may be appropriate. Your auto and homeowners or renters policies provide a certain amount of liability protection, but if you need more, the umbrella coverage kicks in where the others reach their limits. You may have to increase the liability portions of your auto and home coverage to be eligible for the umbrella.

Life insurance

How much life insurance is enough? For a working person who supports a family, the rule of thumb is between five and seven times annual income. But individual needs should always take precedence. Who would suffer financial hardship if you died? (If the answer is no one, you don't need life insurance.) How much money would it take to alleviate that hardship?

The "how much" calculation depends on whether the money would be used to pay off specific amounts, such as a mortgage or other debt, or whether it would need to be invested to provide an income or to cover future expenses. For example, in a traditional young family (the kind that is rare today) with the husband's salary being the only source of income, even if a mortgage was paid off, the wife would need an income to take care of the children, and additional funds would need to be invested to pay for their college education. In all calculations, other investments need to be taken into account too, and life insurance fills the gaps. Because needs change, they should be reviewed periodically.

There is another benefit many life insurance policies offer: an accelerated or terminal illness benefit. If you are diagnosed with a terminal illness and expected to die within six months, you can receive a percentage, usually between 60 and 90 percent of the death benefit, while you are alive. If you survive, you still get to keep the money. The death benefit is reduced proportionally. This type of added coverage doesn't cost more, but not all policies include it.

Aside from determining the amount of life insurance, there

is the question of what type of policy is best, term or "perm," so called because the policy is "permanent." In practice, it keeps going until you reach around age 99, at which point, if you're still alive, you receive the full amount you were insured for. In contrast, buying term insurance means that the insurer agrees to provide the benefit for a fixed premium only for a specified time period, which is usually somewhere between 1 and 20 years. For example, in a ten-year term policy, the premium will be the same for ten years. In year 11, you will usually have the option of renewing the policy regardless of your health, but the cost may be prohibitive if you've reached your fifties or sixties, and the premium will most likely increase each year after that. If you're not in good health, you won't be able to shop around for lower-cost options. And, term coverage usually stops once you've reached age 65 or 70.

The perm policy costs substantially more than term, because it builds a cash value — it's an investment — as well as paying for insurance. There are three types of cash-value policies. Whole Life has fixed premiums; the insurer directs the investment. Universal Life has flexible premiums; the insurer also directs the investment. Variable Life can have fixed or flexible premiums, but you have a choice of investments, including a small group of mutual funds; you can split money between the options and move it around.

Which type of insurance is best for you? There's no pat answer. If you never save a dime but are likely to make your cash-value life insurance payments, such a policy can force you to save. However, it takes time for the cash to build, and if you decide to cancel the policy after a few years, it becomes a losing proposition. During the 1990s, the Consumer Federation of America conducted several surveys of life insurance policies and found that it takes 15 to 20 years to get a reasonably good return on investment.

The argument against building cash value in a life policy is "buy term and invest the rest," meaning invest the difference in premium in something that generates a better rate of return. It sounds good, but unfortunately, many people will never carry out the "invest the rest" part of that strategy. If they don't build up other assets by the time they reach their 50s or 60s, when term insurance gets expensive, they can end up without life insurance and without assets to provide for those they care about, and just their own funeral expenses can be a burden on others. It's a chilling thought, but it happens.

Long term care (LTC) insurance

A relatively new type of coverage, LTC covers in-home care and nursing-home costs as people age and need assistance with day-to-day living. This type of policy is probably the most complex of all insurance. One professional who specializes in LTC coverage estimated that there are over 3,000 possible combinations of benefits for any one individual. Because it relates to several different aspects of life, including your own retirement planning and taking care of others as they age, it is covered in more detail in later chapters.

The Biggest Risk

All insurance is based on "what if" scenarios. If you truly consider the "what if's" that could adversely affect your life and the lives of those you care about, you might well feel pretty miserable. But if you think "what if" you were able to provide adequate financial resources to minimize the hardship of those adverse events, I suspect you'll find it much easier to navigate through the insurance maze.

chapter 8

Places To Put
Your Money

L et's pretend for a moment that there are only two types of people: the rich and the poor. What differentiates one from the other? Money, obviously. The rich have plenty of it, and the poor don't have enough, but from a practical standpoint, that isn't the most important distinction. What is? Their relationship to money. Dollars work for the rich, whereas the poor work for dollars.

Let's consider the richest man in America, Bill Gates. In late 1999, *Forbes* magazine estimated his wealth at $85 billion, yet his annual salary and bonuses, as chairman, CEO and director of Microsoft, totaled only $623,000 in the same year. With that income, it would take about 136,000 years to earn $85 billion, assuming taxes didn't exist. Of course, we know that Gates' real wealth comes from owning a good chunk of Microsoft — about 15 percent — and his wealth fluctuates with the market value of Microsoft stock, which lost over half its value a year after *Forbes'* estimate. (Who's going to complain about being worth only half of $85 billion?) The point is, many people have made fortunes simply by owning a company's stock, without knowing a thing about computers.

When money is put to work, it can reap big rewards. You may well think, "Sure, it's an old story, money makes money. But what if I'm just barely getting by — knowing that other people are getting rich doesn't do me any good." You can certainly stick with that point of view and continue "barely getting by," or consider adopting a new perspective.

Do You Know What Your Dollars Are Doing?

If you had thousands, or even hundreds of people working for you, you would expect to earn a significant amount of money. Well, your dollars are just like a work force, but they may be employed in the wrong jobs, not working hard enough, or even working for someone else at your expense. If you think the last possibility is a bit far-fetched, maybe it is for you, but if you carry any balances on credit cards, take a look at how much you're paying in finance charges, then draw your own conclusions. And if it seems I've overlooked the possibility that some of your dollars are unemployed, I haven't. Your dollars are always doing something, whether you reap any benefits or not.

If you aren't sure where you stand or know you're in a precarious position, realize that you're not alone. A survey by Yankelovich Partners for Minneapolis-based Lutheran Brotherhood found that 21 percent of Americans don't know how much money they have saved; nearly half the population has saved less than $2,500; and of those earning more than $50,000 per year, about one in five has no savings. To size up your own situation, I suggest taking the analogy of dollars-as-employees a step further by assessing what your dollars are doing. Use the worksheet at right or make up your own format, but take a moment to get a sense of your own picture.

Where the Buck Stops

You may feel that you can't choose where your dollars go right now because they're all committed to expenses you can't change. In that case, flip back to Chapter 4, Spending Wisely, and Chapter 5, Use and Abuse of Debt, and find a way to get

during the past year

	Dollars paid in to	Dollars earned (interest, dividends or growth in value)	Dollars lost (interest and finance charges)
Savings			
Retirement account			
Other investments			
Credit card debt			
Other non-mortgage debt			

control of some of your money. The buck really does stop here — with you making a decision, then acting on it.

The issue of money working for you, or vice versa, is the dividing line between having, or not having, options in many aspects of life, such as a job where you spend over one-third of your waking hours (if you work a 40-hour week). Four out of ten people keep a job they don't like for the sake of the money, according to another survey for Lutheran Brotherhood.

Once you decide to put your money to work in your favor, the first urge may be to find exciting places to invest for some of those double-digit annual returns many mutual fund companies advertise. But in many cases, that isn't the most logical way to go, because debt may be eating up substantial double-digit amounts already. If you're paying 20 percent a year in interest, eliminating that debt will earn a 20 percent annual return, guaranteed. Although that may seem too obvious to deserve mention, I meet plenty of people who are surprised to find out that eliminating high-interest debt is their first step in financial planning. On a national scale, surveys by Merrill Lynch over the past ten years have found that managing debt is a priority in financial planning for 72 percent of the population.

The Risk Conundrum

Once debt is under control and you're ready to shop around for the best jobs your dollars can get, the subject of risk becomes the next frontier. There's no way of getting around the fact that risk and reward are intimately related: the more risky an investment, the more returns it may bring (and the key word is "may"). And there is another type of risk: inflation. If your money is in a "safe" place where there is virtually no risk of losing principal but the rate of return is lower than inflation, your dollars are actually losing purchasing power — shrinking — by just sitting there. The only way to deal with risk is to get your own sense of how it works.

Risk and time are inseparable. An investment that is high-risk in the short term may be low-risk in the long run, and the reverse may also hold true. Many people consider the stock market risky, period, but that risk varies, depending on how long money is invested. Although by law, investment results carry the disclaimer, "Past performance is no guarantee of future results," the past does teach us some lessons. If we measure risk by asking "how likely are you to make money, rather than losing it?" history shows that if you allow more time for your money to multiply, you face more favorable odds.

Keep in mind that it isn't possible to invest in "the stock market," because it is a collection of thousands of stocks. The S&P 500 (Standard & Poor's 500 Index) monitors 500 U.S. stocks that are considered to be most representative of the overall market. "Small stocks," or "small caps" (short for "capitalization") are considered in a separate category because their returns are somewhat different. A stock would fall into the "small" category if its capitalization — the number of shares outstanding times the value of each share — falls in the bottom 20 percent of shares listed on the New York Stock Exchange. The fact that these and other categories of stocks tend to gain and lose value at different times adds another dimension to risk. (The different categories of stocks are discussed in Chapter 10.)

Given the complexity of the financial markets, what is the right minimum length of time to invest in stocks? Some financial advisors say at least three to five years, while others say ten. I say it depends on your own attitude toward risk and your over-all financial picture — there isn't any hidden law that gives a magic number.

The Short Term

The value of stock over the longer term is pretty clear, but in a lot of cases, money needs to be saved for the shorter term, as an emergency fund or to make a major purchase. The types of investments that are generally used to produce a gain over a period of a few years or less are bank accounts, either savings or money market accounts; CDs (Certificates of Deposit); or money market funds. Various types of accounts are available at brokerage firms, credit unions and banks. Which type of account and institution is best for you depends on your needs and temperament.

Many people never look beyond their local bank because it seems the safest place for their money. In fact, the FDIC — Federal Deposit Insurance Corporation — insurance, where it applies, has a limit of $100,000 per depositor in a given institution, which could be a bank or a brokerage firm. Similarly, deposits up to $100,000 in credit unions are insured by the National Credit Union Administration, although about three percent of credit unions do not offer this insurance. In all cases, it's best to ask exactly what is insured.

These are some of the ways to store funds for the short term:

- A savings account generally pays the lowest rate of interest and doesn't allow check writing, but funds can usually be accessed with an electronic debit card. Some accounts have monthly fees, some don't, and there is usually no minimum deposit. All are insured by the FDIC.

- A money market account allows limited check writing, with fees for additional checks. Most allow access to funds with an electronic debit card, and some offer automatic payment of your recurring monthly bills. Monthly fees may be charged, depending on the bank and your balance; fees are generally waived if a specified balance is maintained. A minimum deposit, which can be as low as $100 or as high as $50,000, is required to open the account. Interest rates can be significantly higher than with savings accounts, especially with high minimum deposits. These accounts are FDIC insured.

- CDs are FDIC-insured deposits locked in for a specified period of time, anywhere from thirty days to ten years. They can pay rates similar to the high-end money market accounts, and sometimes even higher, for larger deposits and longer time commitments. Although many people consider them very safe, longer-term CDs, after taxes and inflation, are usually a losing proposition. However, they can work well in the short term provided you won't need the money before the maturity date; if you do, there are penalties.

- Money market funds are a type of mutual fund, not a bank account, and are not FDIC insured, but they serve the same purpose, sometimes with better returns. The funds invest in low-risk, short-term debt, and the type of debt they can invest in is regulated by the Securities and Exchange Commission. In effect, these are the lowest-risk mutual funds in existence. By putting money into the fund, you buy shares, which are always valued at $1 each, and you receive earnings as dividends. Checks may be written against your balance, and many of these funds offer electronic debit cards as well. Minimum deposits are usually very low, and your money is not locked in for any period of time, so there is no penalty for withdrawing it at any time.

All of these financial vehicles are designed for storing a chunk of money, even if for a short time, not as a replacement for a regular checking account used for paying day-to-day bills.

Why Shopping Is Complicated

Selecting the best short-term job for your dollars is more complex than ever, and it's only going to get worse, because the lines between banks and brokerages keep getting more and more blurred. No longer are banks the place to go to open bank accounts, and brokerages the place to make investments. Both types of institutions are doing each other's job, creating an overall industry of financial services rather than distinct deposit or investing services. Banks sell investments, and brokerages have started to offer bank accounts, not only the money market type, but regular checking and savings. And CDs are available across the board. Some brokerages also offer credit lines and loans.

All of these institutions want as much of your business as they can get, so they offer perks if you use a combination of their services. For example, if you maintain a certain money market fund or account balance, you may get a free checking account for your day-to-day bill payment, along with free checks. In evaluating your options, the most important thing is to know what you do and don't need. For example, if it's important for you to have a local branch but you can get a better return from an institution that is further away or requires that you make your deposits by mail, you have to decide what's more important. If you're planning to deposit $10,000 for two years, mailing it in may not be such a bad option if you earn a few hundred dollars more in interest.

One question I'm often asked is: "If a CD is FDIC insured and a money market fund is not, why not always stick with the CD?" Because you lock up your money for a preset time in a CD; it isn't liquid. Yes, you can withdraw it early, but penalties will eliminate gains and may even eat into your principal. In many cases, to get a return equal to a money market fund, you may have to lock up your money for a significant period of time. And, the best CD rates demand larger sums. In essence, a money market fund can usually pay you more with much more flexibility and a much smaller balance, and you can usually write checks against it and/or withdraw money with an electronic debit card – valuable features for emergency funds.

Another common question is: "Why not always put money in an FDIC-insured money market account, instead of a fund?" Although money market account dollars are not locked in, as they are in a CD, the other arguments in favor of a fund may apply. For example, you may need a significantly larger balance in the account to avoid monthly fees or to match the rate of return. But, as always, your individual circumstances and temperament take precedence. If you can just see yourself worrying all the time because your fund dollars are not insured, a possible higher return is hardly worth the aggravation.

Aside from flexibility, money market funds have another unique feature: Some of them offer tax-free earnings, because they invest in municipal bonds, and the return on these may not be taxable for you. The catch is, returns on the tax-free types of funds are usually lower than on taxable ones. Deciding which type is best for you is another situation where your personal situation takes precedence.

Investing in Debt

With the accounts above, you're mostly investing in short-term debt such as Treasury Bills – IOUs from the U.S. government for 3, 6 or 12 months. But you can also invest in longer-term debt, which is riskier but can offer a better rate of return. As the name implies, longer-term debt is suitable for longer-term investing.

The federal government offers notes and bonds ranging from two to thirty years in time span, with interest payable at predetermined times. The risk is twofold: the rate of return may not outperform a combination of inflation and taxes, and if you need to cash in the bond before it matures, it does not always sell for its original value, because it is subject to market forces. If interest rates go up after you buy a bond, yours is worth less than one paying a higher rate of interest, so you would have to sell it at a discount or hold onto it for the full term. Each type of government debt has its own minimum investment, ranging from $1,000 to $10,000. You can buy these through banks and brokerages for a fee ranging from $30 to $50, or without fees directly from the federal government, through its Treasury Direct program (see Resources), which has complete information on every type of investment vehicle Uncle Sam offers.

In general, investing in longer-term government debt may be appropriate when receiving a predictable income from a low-risk investment is your priority, such as in retirement. There is also private debt with a full range of risk. In practice, the ins and outs of investing in debt are similar to those of the stock market. Because of the complexity, most individuals today are more likely to invest in mutual funds, which, in turn, invest in various types of debt, or stocks, or a combination of the two. And the subject of mutual funds takes us to the next chapter.

resources

Interest Rates www.bankrate.com
Treasury Direct www.publicdebt.treas.gov

chapter 9

Mutual Funds
Introduction

They're America's most popular investment, next to home ownership, and they just keep growing, and growing, and growing. During the last decade of the old millennium, mutual fund assets increased from $980 million to $5.5 trillion.

What types of people own some of this wealth? They come from all walks of life, according to a survey of more than 1,400 financial decision-makers by the Investment Company Institute (ICI), a national industry association. Over 82 million Americans have a stake in mutual funds, typically about $25,000 per household. About half of fund investors are baby boomers, 22 percent are younger, and the rest were born before 1946. Overall, about half have a college degree.

Do these individuals earn above-average incomes or live off of family trusts? Not according to the ICI survey, which concluded that the typical investor has a regular job and is of "moderate financial means." The median household income among those polled was $55,000, but the majority were married to a spouse who also held a job, so income per person would be significantly lower. And since $55,000 per household is the median, close to half the 82 million investors would be earning considerably less.

These figures support my own observations: that people's saving and investing habits are not determined by their total income. In other words, your nest egg depends on what you do with the money you have rather than the size of your paycheck. And mutual funds offer a simple way to stretch the value of the dollars you set aside, be it for retirement or to achieve other, longer-term financial goals.

Why Mutual Funds Are Attractive

In all my years of advising clients, I've seen one key concern about investing that seems to be uppermost in almost everyone's mind, regardless of their income level or occupation: risk. More specifically, virtually no one wants to take financial risks. I've witnessed this among people of all ages — even among those who take significant risks in business or other activities — even if they consider themselves high-risk takers who get a thrill from some amount of danger (yes, there are exceptions, but they are few and far between).

If I'm to be really accurate, this aversion to "risk" is, in practice, a dislike of volatility. That may seem like a moot point, but it isn't, and hopefully an imaginary scenario will illuminate my case.

Let's pretend that you are asked to invest in a relative's business, say a new hairdressing salon that your niece or nephew, who just graduated from beauty school, dreams of opening. You might fear (quite rationally) that your money will go down the drain because the business will fail and you will never recover a cent, let alone make a profit. That, in the most real sense, is risk. But that isn't what most people are afraid of when they think of investing in mutual funds or individual stocks, because they don't expect big, sometimes very old and established, publicly traded companies to go the way of the niece's or nephew's salon. Happily, their perspective is supported by decades of stock market performance.

So what is "risk" aversion all about? It's an extreme discomfort with volatility, which, in this context, means ups and downs in the value of an asset such as stocks. If you invest $1,000 and the next day it's worth only $975, $950, or even less, it's a very unpleasant experience for most people. Do I enjoy it? Personally, I don't exactly ask Santa Claus to make that sort of thing happen, but when it does (note I didn't say "if"), I don't lose sleep or spend half the day calling my friends to see how their investment is doing and whether they think I should sell right away before I lose any more money. Yet many people react exactly that way.

Let's take a look at the results of a panic approach. Those investors lose a lot of valuable time in what could otherwise be a productive day and, the worst part is, they may follow some "friend's" advice and sell at a loss, only to see that same investment grow handsomely a few weeks later. Then, they conclude their timing was the culprit, try to "time the market," and quite likely get even worse returns.

In contrast, I would seem pretty nonchalant about the same scenario. In fact, I might get excited about an opportunity to buy more of a stock when its value suddenly dropped. I should mention that a fluctuation of 2.5 or 5 percent, in the above example, is not extremely dramatic in today's markets, when the value of high-risk stocks changes much more quickly than in years past. I took a random look at one day's best and worst performers, among individual stocks. As an example, the top gainer that day increased in value by over 60 percent, while the top loser dropped by over 40 percent – in one day. Those are extremes, and I'm talking about single stocks, not diversified mutual funds, but such fluctuations occur.

Am I made of steel? No, but it isn't all that difficult to stay coolheaded if you have realistic expectations. I do have the advantage of familiarity, obviously, as a financial planner. But that doesn't mean I sit and watch the stock market all day long; I couldn't, even if I wanted to (which I don't), because I'm too busy working with my clients. And I certainly don't claim to have any kind of crystal ball. However, I do have a pretty good grasp of longer-term trends, and that's what successful investing is all about.

So what makes mutual funds so attractive? By their very nature, mutual funds offer diversification, or more baskets to put your eggs in. Investors in funds are buying a very small piece of many different stocks and/or bonds, so the ups and downs of one component don't affect the overall value of a fund nearly as much. Since individual investors own shares in a fund's total assets, their shares — which represent the value of their personal investment — don't go up and down as quickly or as dramatically as a single company's stock might.

It's possible to accumulate a personal collection of diversified stocks or bonds, but it's impractical unless you have significant buying power at the outset, which most people don't. And, it would take time and effort to manage such a collection of assets. Mutual funds have managers who do all the work, and the minimum amount you can invest is low enough to enable people of modest means to get started. Where else can you put as little as $25 or $50 a month and, over the years (not necessarily over days or months, or even a year), watch it grow?

One Size Does Not Fit All

Aside from the fact that any one mutual fund enables you to own a tiny piece of a lot of stocks and/or bonds, there are many different types of funds — so many, their names can make your head spin. However, underlying the fancy adjectives, such as "strategic," "special," etc., there are only three basic types — growth, income, and money market. Everything else is either some combination of these or a specialized version of one of them. If you grasp the basic three, you can probably figure out the rest. The following chart shows how the three types stack up in terms of risk, or, in practical terms, the frequency and length of the ups and downs.

potential risk

Growth funds	**HIGHEST RISK**
Income funds	
Money market funds	**LOWEST RISK**

I should mention another key fact about risk, one that, believe it or not, is often overlooked in the face of fear: risk and reward are inseparable. It's unrealistic to expect high returns with low risk; conversely, it would be irrational to take higher risks if higher returns weren't possible. Understanding how the basic types of funds work can alleviate some of the apprehension that, all too often, prevents people from profiting their fair share.

The "Basic Three" at Work

There are two basic ways in which all investments earn money: appreciation, or growth, and income. If you buy a home for $100,000 and later sell it for $125,000, you make $25,000, or a 25-percent return (in very simple terms that ignore costs above and beyond purchase price). If, on the other hand, you keep the house and rent it out, you get income. Similarly, if you buy a stock for $10 and later sell if for $12.50, you also earn 25 percent. There may also be costs associated with owning that stock, which we'll cover in a moment. Or, if the stock pays dividends, you get income, as with the home rental. Bonds, which pay interest, also produce income, and can also appreciate or depreciate in value.

Within the growth and income categories, different types of funds offer a range of risk-reward potential, based on the types of stocks and/or bonds they purchase. Let's look at stocks first. Publicly traded companies attract investors for two reasons: either they offer potential income, as dividends, or they (and the investment community) expect the business to grow, making their shares worth more — appreciate — in the marketplace. Naturally, one single stock can do both, but in practice, many companies rely on growth to produce shareholder profits, while others target dividends.

The difference in approach stems from two different philosophies about rewarding shareholders, and a company's management generally embraces one or the other as its priority. In its most simple form, one theory is that if you pay dividends, less money is left over to reinvest in the business itself, so the company will not grow as quickly. More moderate growth is viewed as a more stable process. Another perspective is, by reinvesting every available dollar to increase its own business, rather than paying dividends, the company will expand its market share and profits more quickly. Then, its stock will — hopefully — be worth more, producing greater gain than the dollars that could have been paid out in dividends.

The growth approach is considered to have the highest earning potential, as well as risk. After all, you as a shareholder must be willing to bet on the company's success and wait for it to come about, without knowing how long that process will take. You deserve to get paid more. Dividends, on the other hand, are generally a more predictable, annual affair.

When it comes to bonds, investors earn money in the form of interest payments, as one might expect, since buying a bond means lending money to its issuer, whether that's the U.S. government, a municipality, or a private company. However, the value of a bond may also fluctuate, especially in the case of longer-term bonds. Let's say you invest $10,000 in a 30-year Treasury bond, which pays 6.5 percent annually in interest. The following year, interest rates go up to 6.75 percent. If you wanted to sell your 6.5-percent issue, no one would pay full value for it, because they can get 6.75-percent issues from the government. In essence, that's why there's a risk when investing in longer-term debt. Short-term debt, which money market funds buy, carries virtually negligible risk. Consequently, debt with a longer time frame brings higher potential returns than its short-term cousin.

Bonds are also issued by private companies who choose to borrow money from investors instead of, or as well as, selling shares in their business. Since these may be riskier propositions than bonds from the U.S. Treasury, they offer proportionally higher rates of return.

The most common hybrids of the basic three types of funds tend to combine elements: growth and income stocks, stocks and bonds ("balanced" funds), and bonds of varied life spans, such as long-term and intermediate bonds. The chart below gives a sense of how they stack up in terms of relative risk, but I must add a word of warning: Before determining if a fund is suitable for your own risk tolerance, you should always examine its prospectus and get competent professional advice if you aren't comfortable making your investment decisions alone.

relative risk and reward potential

Aggressive* growth stock funds	**HIGHEST RISK**
Growth stock funds	
Growth and income funds	
Balanced funds	
Long-term bond funds	
Intermediate- and short-term bond funds	
Money market funds	**LOWEST RISK**

*Aggressive growth stocks are those with the highest potential to appreciate. The companies tend to be younger and/or in industries that are experiencing particularly rapid growth. Since some of these types of companies turn into giants while others perish by the wayside, their risk is high.

Facts and Fallacies

Fact: The biggest investment mistake anyone can make is to never invest any money at all. It's a no-gain proposition, guaranteed, and since we're not talking about body weight here, it's also a no-win situation. That raises the question of where you should invest, whether to use mutual funds, what type, or whether you should consider individual stocks and/or bonds. Why does life have to be so complicated?

The good news is that mutual funds are an easy option, and usually, a less risky one than the alternatives. What's their downside? In recent years, some anti-fund proponents have raised some issues that, at face value, seem to be valid arguments against buying shares in any type of fund, so let's take a look at these.

One argument: "Indexes such as the S&P 500 often perform better than most funds, so why bother with funds that charge fees to manage your money and return less; why not just buy a collection of stocks that mirror the index, or invest in a fund that does the same and charges very low fees?" Whether or not an index outperforms funds that aim to earn more depends on the time frame you examine. As with any numbers, they can be interpreted selectively. If you don't make any attempt to do better than the index, you won't, and there are plenty of funds that have beaten every index there is.

Another argument: "Funds charge too many fees, and you should only buy no-load funds." By law, all fees must be clearly disclosed, and their format is consistent from one fund to another, making it easy to compare. Since there are plenty of sources that explain the fees in great detail, I'm not repeating that material here but have included information on where you can learn more about fees in the Resources section. However, I'd like to address a key point underlying this argument.

If you believe people shouldn't get compensated for the

work they do, then you would expect mutual funds to manage your money, earn great returns, and get paid zero. Not surprisingly, there is no such fund. The expenses you incur when buying and owning mutual fund shares fall into three categories: management of your money; administrative costs; and sales charges or commissions, also known as a "load" which can be paid to people like me when I advise you on financial matters and you decide to invest in a fund through my firm.

Loads are the most contentious issue, and there is a whole community of people who believe you should never pay them. That approach assumes that you never want any professional advice, which is fine if that's your preference. However, if you do want advice but don't get any simply because you don't want to pay for it, it may be one of those "penny wise, pound foolish" situations.

Proponents of anti-load sentiments cite examples of two funds earning the same returns on their investments, but one, because of sales loads and/or higher fees, providing lower real, or net, returns. In a theoretical fund-to-fund comparison, the argument holds water. But — and this is a very big "but" — whenever there is a survey of practical results among real people who invest in funds, the ones who pay a sales load generally get better returns because their behavior as investors is more rational. In essence, people who get professional advice are much less likely to bale out when the value of their investment drops. Instead, they just let it sit there until it recovers and continues to increase, and they profit. In contrast, investors in no-load funds, who receive no help, are much more likely to use the panic strategy, selling at a loss on a down day.

Another common mistake of solo investors is trying to time their investments, rather than investing on a regular basis, regardless of market weather. The timing tends to be after-the-fact. For example, by the time you hear about a stock's fabulous gains on a financial news channel, the hay has probably been made, at least in many cases. Yet novices will buy such a stock, at its new high — the wrong kind of timing. It works the same way with successful mutual funds. As a case in point, after one technology fund announced it's return for 1999, slightly over 200 percent, it received a flood of new investors on January 3, 2000, the first trading day of the year. During the next few days, technology stocks, and that fund, went down, down, down. The people who really benefited were those who invested during the prior year; they experienced the rave results rather than reading about them later in a magazine's list of hot funds.

Successful investing is all about estimating future performance somewhat realistically — making an educated guess about broad swings in trends rather than trying to bet which horse will come first in the fourth race. If you stayed abreast of different industries during the last decade or two and projected that technology was likely to be a winner in the 1990s, you would have been right. (And you would also have known that no market sector keeps going up and up forever. Hopefully, you would have profited by selling at least some of your technology stocks or mutual fund shares while they were still flying high.) But that's what mutual fund managers and their staffs get paid to do.

In practice, fund managers get a much deeper view of a company than folks who subscribe to pricey investment newsletters. Those managers frequently go and meet with executives and employees of companies, check out the premises, get a feel for how the brass thinks and what the employees are really doing — they get to kick the tires, so to speak. I've had the opportunity to meet with many of these people, and I've interviewed quite a few on my TV show, *You And Your Money*. And quite honestly, fund managers really earn their keep. One guy, who manages an international fund that invests in businesses in emerging nations, had to ride a camel to check out a remote facility in a desert, because he wasn't satisfied with just hearing what the top management in a cushy city office had to say. (No, I'm not making that up.)

The bottom line with fees and loads is this: If you get good value, as in good advice and good management of your money, the cost is worth every penny. If the advice is bad or nonexistent, or if the management is poor . . . well, maybe it's time to switch.

resources

The Investment Company Institute www.ici.org

The members of this national association, mutual funds and other types of investment companies provide an overview of the fund world.

U.S. Securities and Exchange Commission www.sec.gov

The regulatory body of the U.S. investment industry explains its role and all the legal resources available to investors.

chapter 10

Retirement Plans and Mutual Funds

Building a retirement nest egg is the most common goal of mutual fund investors, and employer-sponsored retirement saving plans such as the 401k are the most popular vehicle. It isn't surprising, given the tax advantages and, often, matching funds from employers. Nearly nine out of ten employers with 401k plans match employee contributions, most often 50 cents to each employee dollar, up to a maximum of 6 percent of an individual's salary, according to Buck Consultants, a New York-based benefit consulting firm. A 50-percent return, even before you earn a dime from investments, is a great deal! So how come there haven't been any stampedes (at least not that I've heard of) to drop every possible dollar into 401k plans?

To be fair, the number of people saving for retirement is growing, but not quickly enough. Almost half of retirees age 60 and older rely on Social Security as their biggest source of income, according to research cosponsored by the Employee Benefit Research Institute (EBRI), a nonprofit research organization in Washington, D.C. And, a Merrill Lynch survey of about 900 working individuals found that almost nine out of ten worked for companies that offer a retirement plan, but only 58 percent of those eligible made any contributions at all, let alone the maximum allowed.

Is there some secret path to retirement riches I don't know about? It seems not. The EBRI study, which polled approximately 1,000 people, found that only one in four Americans feels very confident about having enough money to live comfortably in retirement, and even then, researchers concluded that much of this optimism is ill-founded, because it isn't backed up by sound planning and action. Other research shows that more and more people are never planning to retire completely, but intend to work at least part-time, mostly for financial reasons.

Given these trends, the traditional starting point for retirement planning — working out how much income you will need and how much must be saved between now and then — seems removed from reality in many situations. For many people, there simply isn't enough time — or enough current income to make up for lost time — to achieve the ideal. So rather than focusing on how to calculate the income you will need down the road (see this chapter's Resources for tools to do this), I'm going to look at the key things you have to know to take positive steps to build the best retirement future possible. Fortunately, it's never too late to turn the wheel in a better direction, and the first step is considering available opportunities.

What a Retirement Plan Isn't

In and of itself, a retirement plan — such as a 401k or an IRA — is not an investment but a place where your money is protected from taxes. Think of it as a coat. It protects you against the cold, so that you can go places, but simply wearing it doesn't mean you will go anywhere, unless you start walking.

Let's take a look at the 401k, an opportunity that is significantly underutilized. (There are other options if this one isn't available to you, but the underlying principles are the same.) If you "put money into your 401k," the IRS considers that you are "deferring" that portion of your income. In other words, you are choosing not to pocket it today. Instead, you are placing it in a special piggy bank so that you will have a nest egg to support yourself in later years. The theory is, because you are making an effort to be financially self-sufficient down the road, you are rewarded by not having to pay taxes on that money now.

There are reasons why both the government and employers encourage you to save this way. Although Social Security is not likely to disappear in the near future, it also isn't likely to provide you with enough income to live comfortably. For employers, life is easier if they don't have to pay you a guaranteed pension for the rest of your life. (Even if you will receive a pension, why turn down an opportunity to have more?)

When you "defer" a portion of your income by putting it into a 401k, that amount is subtracted from your taxable income, saving you some money on the spot. If you invest your dollars, you won't be taxed on your profits either, but naturally, there's a catch. If you decide to take any money out of your tax-protected piggy bank before reaching age 59½, you will pay a 10-percent penalty, plus you will be taxed on the full amount you withdraw, with some special exceptions (see Retirement Saving Rules chart later in this chapter). Once you turn 59½, funds you withdraw will be taxed as income but without a penalty.

The upshot is that by allowing your money to grow without being taxed along the way, you accumulate much more (to compare, flip back to the chart in Chapter 6, How Taxes Impact the Growth of Your Savings). But the key word is "grow." Wearing a tax-protected coat doesn't magically make your dollars multiply; you have to invest them somewhere, and your choice makes a big difference.

Piggy-Bank Management Trends

While not putting any money at all into a retirement plan is the biggest mistake, not letting it grow — by investing too conservatively — is a close runner-up. A study by the National Bureau of Economic Research compared returns on the same amount invested two different ways over 30 years: half in stocks and half in bonds in one case and all in stocks in the other. The all-stock investment grew to roughly double the more conservative portfolio. While it isn't true that all money should always be invested in stocks, people have a tendency to err on the conservative side during the years when their money needs to work hard, mistakenly believing that they are doing the right thing.

Repeated surveys of employees' investment behavior with their 401k funds shows that lack of education is the biggest barrier to smart investment decisions. And where employers have provided more education, employees have invested more in growth funds. Over the years, I have also found that knowledge empowers my clients to make decisions that reap the biggest financial rewards. And I've noticed that 401k plans are offering more and more investment options, making greater familiarity with them a necessity.

Not-So-Common Knowledge

The idea that it's prudent to diversify is not new, but it's often misunderstood, and I've found that the misconceptions fall into two main categories: Thinking you're diversified when you're not and diversifying in a way that unnecessarily limits growth. Both stem from a lack of knowledge about how different types of investments — or market sectors — work. I'll look at these in terms of mutual funds, since they parallel the financial world overall.

Let's assume you've invested in several stock mutual funds — you're diversifying, right? Not necessarily. If all those mutual funds buy the same types of stocks, your eggs are actually in one basket. I've met people who invested in several different mutual fund families, such as Fidelity, Vanguard and T. Rowe Price, and were confident as can be about their diversification.

However, a closer look revealed that the top holdings in all three funds were nearly identical. If you invest in three different funds and each one has a major stake in Intel stock, you've simply bought Intel through three different intermediaries. That may sound like a no-brainer, but in the real world, it's a common mistake made by plenty of intelligent people.

The other common mistake is selecting funds that truly are diversified but unnecessarily limit your growth potential. Most often this happens when an individual really needs to target growth investments but puts too much money into bond — or income — funds. These are good places to put money when you need income — usually when retirement is closer at hand or has already arrived — but not when you need your money to grow for the future. This type of mistake poses the very real risk of not earning enough returns for a comfortable retirement.

So how do you diversify the right way — to reduce risk in the true sense? Success requires knowing how different types of mutual funds work and what a given fund does and doesn't do.

Getting the Important Facts

Although people talk about "the market" going up or down, that phrase breeds misunderstanding because in practice, different types of stocks follow different patterns of highs and lows. And while I can't claim to describe all the nuances here, being aware of these fundamental categories is a good starting point:

■ **Growth**

Funds purchase stocks that are increasing in value and are expected to keep climbing.

■ **Value**

Funds look for growth stocks whose value has dropped for some reason, buy and wait for them to rebound.

■ Large cap

Funds concentrate on companies with large capitalization, technically those with outstanding shares worth $2 billion or more.

■ Small cap

Funds buy stocks of small-capitalization companies, generally those whose total shares are worth $1 billion or less.

The key thing about these categories of funds is that each one has its own pattern of ups and downs, making it unlikely that all will be up or down at the same time. Because no one has ever figured out how to time the market perfectly, investing some of your money in each type gives you an opportunity to profit from more peaks and to offset downturns when those occur.

How do you tell which category a given fund belongs to? Its name tells part of the story, but you also have to look at the fund prospectus — an experience that can be daunting if you don't know what to look for. Fortunately, getting a grasp of what a fund does is not all that difficult if you look in two places in that document: the fund's objective and its top ten holdings.

If you can't fathom what the objective means, ask your investment advisor, if you have one, or call the fund directly. Either way, you should be able to get questions answered to your satisfaction. Looking at the top ten holdings and the percentage of each should also give you a good picture of what the fund is about. Comparing these two elements should give you a good idea of the differences and similarities between funds.

In addition to the above terms, the following merit some explanation because they often create confusion:

■ Global

Funds hold stocks in foreign companies as well as domestic ones and may be made up of predominantly U.S. stocks.

■ International

Funds buy stocks in non-U.S. companies only.

■ Foreign

Funds may or may not include U.S. companies.

In each case, looking at the fund's objectives and top holdings is the only way you can get a sense of how it works. And most important, your choice of funds should parallel your personal objectives. If you have decades before retirement and want aggressive growth, your fund should aim to achieve that. In contrast, if you're on the verge of retirement, you will want to preserve what you have and start receiving some income soon, while maintaining some growth to ensure sufficient assets for future income.

Keep in mind that funds are managed by human beings, and although every fund manager has a staff of researchers and is obligated to make choices within the boundaries set by the fund's objectives, each one also has a personal style — something that is difficult to ascertain by reading a prospectus.

I have been fortunate in having the opportunity to speak at length with many managers, as a host of the *You and Your Money* television show and while doing due diligence on the funds I represent as a financial planner. I have learned that individuals' methods vary quite a bit. On one end of the spectrum, there are managers who base buying and selling decisions strictly on mathematical formulas; on the other end, there are those who rely quite a bit on their own intuition, even if it is a well educated type of intuition supported by research and disciplined by the boundaries a fund's objectives impose. How can you glean some insight into a manager's personal style? Some funds make information about their managers available to investors; you may find interviews with managers in the media or on a fund family's Web site. Or, you may just want to stick to the nuts-and-bolts information in the prospectus.

A Word about Insurance

Unlike FDIC-insured bank accounts, the money you invest in mutual funds is not protected against market fluctuations. In other words, there is no guarantee that your principal won't decline when the value of stocks or bonds declines. This is true even if you invest in mutual funds through a bank. However, the Securities Investor Protection Corporation insures accounts of member brokerages against failure of the brokerage, up to $500,000 per account.

Retirement Plan Summary

While 401k plans are the most prevalent type of retirement plan today — and one to take advantage of if it's available to you — they are only one of numerous options summarized at right. In each case, you decide how your money will be invested. Some employer-sponsored plans offer a small range of investment choices while others offer many more. Whether you have a choice of a few only or literally any mutual fund available, as well as individual stocks and bonds, is determined by the employer. In each type of plan, tax regulations allow you to invest in all types of publicly traded securities.

In all cases except the Roth IRA, 100 percent of tax-deductible contributions and earnings are always taxed as ordinary income when you withdraw money. Penalties are charged in addition to income taxes. There are also penalties for not withdrawing enough money once you reach age 70½, in all cases but the Roth, which is discussed in a later chapter.

The Critical Elements

Regardless of your age and financial means, there is only one way to build for a retirement: Make a decision, learn enough about your options to find a way to improve your situation in the future, then do everything you can in that direction.

retirement saving rules

Plan	Who sets it up	Annual contribution limit*	Penalty for with-drawal before age 59½**
401k	Corporations	Within limits set by the employer and tax codes, you choose a percentage of your salary to defer to your 401k. The employer may match your contributions. Maximum contributions: 2002: $11,000/$12,000 2003: $12,000/$14,000 2004: $13,000/$16,000 2005: $14,000/$18,000 2006: $15,000/$20,000	10%
403b	Tax-exempt institutions such as government and nonprofit agencies	As for the 401k	10%
SEP-IRA	Self-employed individuals and small businesses with up to 10 employees	15% of compensation or $30,000, whichever is less	10%
SIMPLE-IRA	Self-employed individuals and small businesses with 100 or fewer employees	Employers are required to contribute either 2% of compensation to all employees or make a match of 3% of compensation, up to the maximum, to participating employees. Maximum employee contributions (not a percentage of salary): 2002: $7,000/$7,500 2003: $8,000/$9,000 2004: $9,000/$10,500 2005: $10,000/$12,500 2006: $10,000/$12,500	25% for with-drawals in the first two years; 10% thereafter

continued on next page

retirement saving rules _{continued}

Plan	Who sets it up	Annual contribution limit*	Penalty for withdrawal before age 59½**
Keogh	Self-employed individuals, partnerships and small companies	25% of compensation or $30,000, whichever is less	10%
Traditional IRA	Individuals	Contributions may or may not be tax-deductible, but earnings are not taxed while they grow. To tax deduct contributions, your adjusted gross income must fall under amounts specified each year by the IRS. Maximum contributions: 2002: $3,000/$3,500 2003: $3,000/$3,500 2004: $3,000/$3,500 2005: $4,000/$4,500 2006: $4,000/$5,000	10% on all tax-deductible contributions and earnings
Roth IRA	Individuals	You are eligible if your adjusted gross income falls below limits specified each year by the IRS. Contributions are not tax-deductible, but your investments grow tax-free and you may withdraw earnings tax-free after 59½ as long as your account has been open at least five years. Principal may be withdrawn any time without penalties. Maximum contributions: as for the Traditional IRA.	10% on earnings only

* Annual dollar amounts are for under age 50/age 50 and older individuals.

** Some 401k and 403b plans allow loans for specified reasons, and both these plans and IRAs allow early withdrawals without penalties in some situations, such as the purchase of a first home, medical expenses that exceed a certain amount, some educational expenses and others. Always consult with a tax advisor before deciding to make an early withdrawal; consider all your options and alternative sources of money.

A STEP-BY-STEP GUIDE TO FINANCIAL BLI$$

resources

Choose to Save www.choosetosave.org

A service of the Employee Benefit Research Institute, the site includes more than 100 online calculators to help you identify amounts needed for retirement.

Internal Revenue Service www.irs.gov

The official source of information about regulations governing contributions to and withdrawals from retirement plans.

chapter 11

Life Stages I – Growing Your Money

Money management and time are joined at the hip. What makes an investment better or worse — whether it's for your retirement nest egg, a down payment on a home or a college fund — is a function of the clock more than any other factor. And when it comes to money, the old guy with the scythe can be on your side for a change, if you know how to harness the power.

My optimism stems partially from the fact that people are living longer. The 85-plus segment is growing faster that any other age group, although this fact is not widely known. A survey of over 2,000 adults for the American Association of Retired Persons (AARP) found that overall, only 28 percent were aware of this trend, and among 18- to 24-year-olds, only 13 percent knew. In addition, there are now over 70,000 people in this country who are 100 years old or older, nearly double the number in 1990. By 2050, the Census Bureau estimates that we will have between 265,000 and 4.2 million centenarians.

Sadly, the AARP survey also found that only 27 percent of those polled wanted to live for as long as an entire century. Their greatest worries were poor physical health (among 46 percent of respondents) and lack of money (among 38 percent). However, between advances in the treatment of disease and what we know today about prevention — how nutrition, exercise and lifestyle influence our physical well-being — a longer life can also be a healthy one. And when it comes to money, a longer lifespan offers more opportunity as well as a greater challenge. No one wants to outlive his or her money.

The younger you are, the more time there is for your money to work. (It is also quite striking how a difference of 2 percent in annual returns adds up over time.)

when time is on your side

Amount/time invested in an IRA (returns are rounded to the nearest $1,000)	Total, earning 8% annual return	Total, earning 10% annual return
$2,000 annually from ages 25-34, then left to accumulate until age 65	$315,000	$612,000
$2,000 annually from ages 35-65	$245,000	$362,000

Life being the way it is, there are always obstacles to achieving goals, and being younger doesn't mean there aren't very real challenges to starting a long-term investment program. Chief among these is one's perception of the longer-term future. Very few people think about retirement early in life, and there are other, much more appealing places to put money. Apart from possible obligations, such as repaying student loans, there are houses and cars to buy, vacations to take and families to raise. These are all valid places to spend money (for ideas on how to cut down everyday expenses dramatically, see Resources at the end of this chapter), but the value of investing some of it for the longer haul cannot be underestimated.

The Key Building Blocks

If you pay any attention to financial news, you'll hear plenty about the hottest stocks and big market swings, up or down. Yet those facts have little to do with investing your money wisely. What does? Asset allocation. The subject isn't considered sexy enough to warrant much media attention, or even much coverage on Web sites, yet it lies at the heart of every successful investment strategy.

Asset allocation is, in essence, a set of rules that determines what portion of your portfolio is in different types of stocks, bonds or cash (generally kept in CDs or money market funds). You — and your financial advisor if you have one — set the rules to fit your personal situation and goals, but there are some underlying principles that savvy investors use.

To get a sense of why such rules are worth bothering with, let's look at your refrigerator for a moment. What if it were full of ice cream and nothing else? You buy different types of food for different uses: breakfast, lunch, dinner, snacks and desserts, and beverages. When you shop for food, you take that into account and may even shop at different stores for specific items. If someone had no familiarity with our food, they might just fill up their refrigerator with ice cream, or try drinking hot sauce when they're thirsty — after all, it looks a lot like tomato juice. Asset allocation is very much like stocking your refrigerator to make sure that the next time you're thirsty, there's something to drink besides hot sauce.

In practice, the returns you get on your money are influenced much more by categories of assets you invest in than by hot stock picks. And there are general rules of thumb for different stages of life or time horizons. In essence, the longer you plan to keep money invested, the more risk you can afford to take, because you have time to wait out downswings in the market. Since growth stocks, as a category, can be expected (although there's no guarantee) to increase in value in the longer term, longer-term investors face much less risk than those who must have their money available at short notice.

If your twenties are long gone but you aren't financially set for retirement, it's never too late to start, and you're not alone.

Perhaps you need to plan working for more years, but rather than feeling that all is lost, realize that learning the basics and using them is still the key to a better financial future. If you're older, you have the advantage of recognizing the importance of building a nest egg, and as long as you use that knowledge to motivate yourself to take action, the future may be brighter than you expect.

Identifying Asset Categories

During the last century, many financial experts have crunched numbers to examine "what if" investment scenarios based on historical performance of markets. Among other things, their efforts have produced some interesting tidbits: If George Washington had invested one dollar in growth stocks, his heirs would have been millionaires seven times over before anyone ever   heard of publicly traded technology or biotech businesses.

Number crunching has also illustrated some practical information. Although the past doesn't forecast the future, a hundred years of experience does count for something, and it   boils down to this: If your objective is to grow your dollars over a span of 10 to 15 years or more, investing most of your money in growth stocks offers the best investment opportunity.

There is another, equally important trend: The category of "growth stocks" breaks down into smaller categories, including but not limited to large-cap, small-cap, foreign and value stocks in these categories. Distributing your stock investments among different types of stocks gives you an opportunity to take advantage of upswings in all of them and minimizes the effects of downturns in a given category. In a nutshell, it's almost impossible to "time" these categories — always buy low and sell high. Experience shows that by trying to time purchases and sales, you're most likely to buy high and sell low. However, if you're already in different categories, then you take advantage of the ups, and when one goes down, the others even out the shock.

The chart below illustrates some of the differences in performance of mutual funds among these categories and includes some bond information for comparison.

Setting Your Own Rules

Conventional wisdom says that with a longer time span, about 80 percent of a portfolio should be invested in growth stocks, especially smaller, more aggressive ones. For the remainder, it is generally recommended that 15 percent should be in bonds, with 5 percent in a money market account. However, there is no cast-in-stone ratio. Some experts recommend 100 percent in stocks, with a 15-year-plus horizon, while others say always put at least 40 percent in bonds. Sound confusing? It is. Ultimately, the choice is yours, and I can't recommend a cookie-cutter ratio. I do suggest that you get acquainted with your options, either

average returns of different categories of mutual funds listed on Nasdaq

Mutual fund category	4-week*	Average annual returns				Best fund**	Worst fund**
		1-year	3-year	5-year	10-year		
Large-cap growth	-9.9%	23.1%	30.7%	26.2%	18.7%	129.7%	2.1%
Small-cap growth	-24.2%	46.7%	27.2%	18.8%	16.8%	156%	-1.3%
Large-cap value	1.6%	0.8%	16.7%	19.1%	15.1%	21.9%	-21.7%
Small-cap value	-4.5%	11.1%	7.4%	12.2%	12.0%	143.6%	-16.2%
General U.S. government bond	0.8%	0.5%	5.8%	6.0%	7.1%	5.9%	-3.9%

* Average return during a randomly selected 4-week period
** Best/worst annual return for a single mutual fund in a recent 1-year period

through an advisor or by doing some homework, and I've included some sources of more detailed information in the Resources section at the end of this chapter.

Once you have decided on the stock ratio for your own portfolio and have decided on categories of stock, it takes a little diligence to follow those rules. As a simple example, let's say you start out with a lump sum of $100,000 and invest 80 percent in stock funds, 15 percent in bond funds and 5 percent in a money market fund. Since stock does grow faster than the other categories of investments, the ratio will change. If you follow your own rules, you will move some of your stock earnings into bonds and money markets to maintain your 80-15-5 ratio.

In other words, practicing the discipline of asset allocation takes more work than meets the naked eye, and there's even more to it. If your money is in a retirement account where your gains are not currently taxable, that's the end of the story. However, any other investments have tax liabilities when you sell them, and depending on your personal situation, it may not be prudent to sell the instant your ratios are out of kilter. Now it's getting really complicated, I know, but it wouldn't be fair on my part to mislead you by ignoring the real world. The most critical thing to remember about possible tax consequences is to make sure you have all the documentation you ever received regarding your investments, including what you bought when and for how much, and consult with a tax advisor before making changes.

The complexity of sorting through the options and their consequences is a major reason why people get financial planning advice, above and beyond tax guidance. Some mutual fund companies have started to offer a solution, too, by creating funds designed for different stages of life. In essence, the fund does the asset allocation for you and shifts things around to keep a ratio in tact. There are a couple of drawbacks to this alternative: It changes your tax liability if the investment is outside a tax-deferred retirement plan and gives you less control over how you might minimize taxes on gains. Plus, since there are only a limited number of these types of funds, your choices are limited, and that may mean you lose some gains in the long run. Regardless of how you choose to work, if you have a grasp of the basic principles, you will be further ahead.

Category Pitfalls to Avoid

In addition to large/small cap, value, foreign and other categories, many mutual funds specialize in or favor certain industries within their category. If one or more of your funds end up holding a lot of their assets in a single industry, be aware that your risk increases because industries also experience ups and downs.

During the spring of 2000, for example, the wireless communications industry was second in a *Wall Street Journal* list of the ten best-performing over periods of one and five years, returning approximately 98 and 608 percent during those time periods, respectively. However, when the stock market experienced a downturn at that time, a one-week rating of the ten best- and worst-performing industries placed wireless communications in the number-two spot among the losers, with a one-week loss of over 16 percent. In contrast, coal made the top-ten one-week best-performing list — with a 4.5 percent increase — after leading the ten worst over a five-year period with a loss of over 62 percent.

Countries and regions of the world also experience their own up and down markets. As a rule, it is very risky to invest in a fund that is country-specific. Somewhat less risky are region-specific funds, such as Europe or Asia, with more diversified foreign funds posing the least risk in the breed. With the latter, however, assets of a fund may become concentrated in one country or region over a period of time, and unless you keep a watchful eye on its top ten holdings, you may end up with more risk than you expected.

Dealing with the Complexities

Needless to say, money management requires a considerable amount of vigilance. By investing in mutual funds, you are assigning some of that job to the fund manager — how much depends on the types of funds and fund families you choose.

Some funds have more narrowly defined objectives, while others have more flexible parameters, leaving the manager with a wider variety of choices. For example, one large-cap fund may invest strictly in large-cap stocks, while another may invest predominantly in large companies but has the flexibility to invest in companies of all sizes. There may be a minimum or maximum percentage of assets that will be invested in companies of a certain size, or not. These issues are addressed in the prospectus of a fund, and since prospectuses today are written in pretty straightforward language, the overall objective of a fund and the degree to which it invests in a variety of categories of stock should be clear.

Granted, it may take you a while to get used to evaluating funds, but if you get prospectuses from a number of funds and fund families and compare, the trees should become identifiable in the forest. I do suggest that you look at more than one fund family, since some of these tend to have a certain style that permeates their funds. Ultimately, if you don't want to do any of this, you have to get professional advice. Even if you do, having a better grasp of the subject will always work in your favor.

A Word about Timing

I've made the point that trying to time the market works against most people most of the time, but there is a different type of timing that does work: dollar cost averaging. I recommend this approach only if you are saving and investing a set amount of money on a regular basis, such as weekly or monthly, not if you are investing a lump sum. It works very well if you put a set percentage of every paycheck into a 401k, for example.

Dollar cost average is a discipline whereby you invest the same amount regularly, regardless of what the price of a stock or mutual fund share is doing. In other words, rather than trying to buy a set number of shares each month, you buy however many shares a set dollar amount will buy. Why? Because you end up paying less per share in the long run.

Here's an example:

dollar cost averaging

Time period (weekly, monthly, etc.)	Amount invested	Price of shares	Number of shares purchased
1	$300	25	12
2	$300	75	4
3	$300	50	6
4	$300	60	5
Average price per share:		$52.50	
Average price paid using dollar cost averaging:		$44.44	

It really works with mutual funds rather than individual stocks, because you can't buy a fraction of a stock, but you can buy any fraction of a fund share.

Keeping Your Asset Allocation on Track

I've been discussing asset allocation for the stage of life where growing your money is the priority. As the years go by, priorities change — eventually you will be withdrawing some of your earnings for income, which you want to last for the rest of your life. Shifting your emphasis from long-term growth to income cannot be done overnight; it also requires a longer-term view and plan. And that process brings us to the next chapter.

resources

For money-saving strategies

www.frugalfamilynetwork.com

www.frugalliving.about.com

For more information about asset allocation

www.efficientfrontier.com

www.sensible-investor.com

chapter 12

Life Stages II – Nest Egg Hatching

T he concept of saving for the future is pretty simple. You save and save and save, then one day you start spending. But as with asset allocation, there's more to it in practice, so much so that shifting into spending mode requires even more foresight than investing for growth (unless you are in the very small minority of people with bottomless pockets).

Topping the list of challenges in planning for the spending phase of your life is the time element — you don't want to outlive your money but you do want to collect as much as possible. Your chances of achieving both of these objectives increase with sound planning, which should begin at least ten years before you expect to start dipping into any part of your nest egg — including Social Security benefits, a company pension, retirement savings and other investments, plus any other possible sources of income. These are some of the reasons why it's vital to look ahead:

- If you have invested for the long haul, in growth stocks or funds, market swings can be expected, and you don't want to be forced to sell assets when their value is down. The risk of doing so is very real if you don't start planning withdrawals soon enough.
- If you are eligible for a company pension, your last few years' earnings generally have a big impact on the value of

benefits after you retire, and many employers offer early retirement options with reduced benefits. If you are not fully aware of how your pension benefits are calculated, you may make some decisions that are more costly than you expect.

- As you approach retirement age, you may have more disposable income than you've ever had, and the idea of investing it all in aggressive growth stocks or funds may seem very appealing, but it's the wrong strategy at this stage.
- A reality check with at least ten full-time working years ahead of you leaves some time to make changes if you're not on track for the retirement lifestyle you had hoped for.

Retirement Expectations

The American vision of retirement isn't what it used to be. Eight in ten baby boomers expect to work during their retirement years, at least part-time. Of those, over half anticipate doing so because they need the income, while the others want to work for other reasons.

These findings, from a survey of 2,000 boomers for AARP, point to a very different future from the golf-course or sail-boat types of retirement scenes idolized by earlier generations. I suspect that part of the change stems from the expectation of longer, healthier lifespans, and part from a changing perspective on work being an interesting or enjoyable activity, rather than a necessary evil.

Regardless of why or how the concept of retirement is changing, the fact that it is changing creates different needs for retirement nest eggs. The basic principles of investing don't change, but their application becomes more complex.

Traditional Life-Stage Investing

Let's pretend for a moment that retirement follows the traditional full-time work to no-work pattern. Then we'll see how the same principles can be applied to the kind of situation most baby boomers will likely experience, with some income from work and some from retirement savings.

To avoid outliving one's money, a nest egg has to meet two objectives during retirement: capital preservation, so that you don't run out of principal; and income, so that you have money to live on. In the years approaching retirement, an investment portfolio should undergo a process of gradual transformation to shift from its earlier objective of growth into preservation-and-income mode.

Although each individual's situation is unique, the general rules to achieve this shift have been to move assets, bit by bit, from more- to less-volatile investments, and from those designed for growth to ones designed to produce ongoing income. The classic age-related portfolios look something like this:

Life stage of investor	Stocks	Bonds	Cash*
Young	80%	15%	5%
10 years to retirement	60%	30%	10%
5 years to retirement	40%	40%	20%
* Money market funds or accounts and CDs			

In addition to shifting money from stocks to bonds and cash, these traditional types of portfolios shift the stock portion from more aggressive growth stocks into less risky and dividend-paying stocks as the clock ticks forward.

What happens after retirement? Once upon a time, retirees avoided growth stocks all together, putting their money in bonds, CDs, savings accounts and perhaps blue-chip, dividend-paying stocks, for maximum safety of principal. Unfortunately, that strategy had a major flaw in that it ignored inflation, which has run higher than savings accounts and short-term CDs, and even stock dividends at times. As a result, the purchasing power of nest eggs shrank. History taught us a valuable lesson: that the "safe" investments are not so safe after all. Now, it's considered mandatory for a retiree's portfolio to include some growth stocks to outpace inflation.

The Basics of Nest-Egg Spending

Given that most future retirees will have a combination of income sources, ongoing work being one, it's impossible to invent cookie-cutter portfolios. The possible combinations of factors in individual lives are almost endless. Consequently, there is no escaping the need to understand the fundamentals of planning for nest-egg spending, even if you get professional advice.

There are four main factors to consider.

1 | **Growth stocks are long-term investments.**
Remember the rule about growth investing — it's realistic to expect growth stocks to increase in value, historically averaging about 10 percent per year, if you don't need your money for about ten years or more. As your time horizon shortens, money needs to be moved into less volatile investments, to avoid having to cash in assets when they are at a low point. If we think of small-cap growth stocks as the most aggressive and risky, the other end of the spectrum would be short-term government bonds and CDs, with large-cap stocks and longer-term bonds in between.

2 | **Growth stocks don't produce a stream of income.**
These assets are true to their name in that investors profit when they buy at a lower price, wait for the value to grow, then sell for a higher price. If you try to do this in a short time frame, the risk of losing a significant part of your principal becomes very high. Higher-risk stocks still have a place in retirement years, to fuel the growth of principal and outpace inflation, but only in that portion of a portfolio that will remain invested for some years to come.

3 | Dividend-paying stocks produce income.

Stocks that are issued by large, stable companies, pay dividends and have relatively little volatility offer ongoing income.

4 | Bonds can produce income.

Some bonds offer regular interest payments and are virtually risk free, while others pose high risk.

The Bond World

The risk spectrum of bonds is just as broad as that of stocks, although the ups and downs of the bond market do not follow the overall pattern of stocks because interest-rate fluctuations affect these two markets in opposite ways.

When interest rates rise, governments and companies issuing new bonds have to offer higher rates of return to attract investors. This makes bonds more desirable, and therefore more valuable, and the relative value of stocks drops. When interest rates drop, the opposite happens.

Interest fluctuations also have a major impact on bonds already in circulation, because bonds are traded, like stocks. When interest rates rise, older bonds that pay lower rates drop in value. When interest rates drop, older bonds paying higher rates become more valuable. Longer-term bonds are more risky because there is a longer time span during which interest rates will change. Consequently, at the time they are issued, longer-term bonds usually offer a higher rate than shorter-term ones.

Bonds or Bond Funds for Income?

The theory that it is less risky to invest in stock funds rather than individual stocks — because a fund offers diversification — does not necessarily hold true when it comes to bonds. Here's why:

- With an individual bond, the principal will be repaid in full, plus interest — if the issuer is a stable one, such as the federal government. In a mutual fund, there are no guarantees of principal and there is no predetermined, guaranteed rate of interest for a preset time period, yet these are essential elements for a predictable income.

- A money market fund, which invests in short-term debt only, is the safest and most predictable type of fund but generally offers a too low a rate of interest for retirement needs.

- Aside from money market funds, bond funds generally produce earnings both by trading bonds and collecting interest, so the value of the fund's shares go up and down, quite dramatically in riskier funds. This poses the same problem as growth-stock funds — you may have to cash in shares when their value is down, depleting your principal. (There are funds which buy bonds and hold them to maturity, but these are a special category — generally called "target maturity funds" — not the majority.)

Given these factors, it's important to realize that different bonds and bond funds can serve different purposes. Some mutual funds are designed to provide current income, and although they may not be right for all situations, they certainly provide a simple option.

Two Ways Bonds Pay

If you want to invest in bonds to guarantee your principal and receive a predictable income, the most logical choice is government bonds. Aside from safety, there are tax benefits. States don't tax earnings on federal government bonds, and the federal government doesn't tax earnings on municipal — or muni — bonds. In many cases, states don't tax muni earnings either.

Although all bonds pay interest, they do it in two different ways, depending on whether or not they have a "coupon." This term is used because all bonds once literally had a coupon which the holder tore off and turned in for each interest payment. The actual tear-off coupons mostly disappeared over time, but the word lingers.

When a bond has a "coupon," you receive interest on a regular basis, most often semiannually. A zero-coupon bond works differently. You buy it at a discount and receive full value at maturity. The difference is equal to the stated interest over the life of the bond. The down side is that whatever tax is due must be paid each year you earn the theoretical interest, even though you don't see any cash. However, you will have a windfall when the bond matures, with only the last year's earnings to pay tax on.

Given the complexity of choices when it comes to bonds, there is no way of avoiding the need to become familiar with this world. That's the only way you can make sure that your individual financial picture and needs will be served well.

Withdrawing Money from Retirement Plans

Uncle Sam allows you to accumulate and grow money in retirement plans without paying taxes along the way, but when you start to withdraw income, there are some very specific rules to follow. On top of a 10-percent penalty for withdrawing money before age 59½, there are much stiffer penalties for leaving money in too long. When you reach age 70½, if you don't withdraw a required minimum amount, you will pay a 50-percent excise tax on the shortfall every year. This holds true even if you are still working full-time, with one exception: If your retirement funds are in a 401k sponsored by your employer at that time, there are no minimum required withdrawals. However, once you retire, you have to start withdrawing the required minimums by April 1 of the year following the one in which you retire. This exception does not apply to IRAs.

How much do you have to take out? An amount the IRS specifies per a formula that is far too complex for most mortals, so you need a competent tax professional to figure it out before you reach 70½. However, I can explain the rationale underlying the magic numbers. The dollars you must withdraw each year from your retirement plan, in roughly equal amounts, are supposed to be an amount that enables the money to last just as long as you live, but no longer, at least in theory. The IRS provides life expectancy tables for the calculations. You pay income tax on your withdrawals each year, unless they're coming out of a Roth IRA or an IRA where your contributions were after-tax dollars, in which case you need a pro again to calculate your tax liability, because you still have to pay taxes on your earnings, but not on the after-tax dollars you originally invested.

Once you've reached 59½, what about taking out all the money from a retirement plan in one shot? You can do that, and if it's a 401k and you're retiring at age 55, you can also do that (this doesn't apply to an IRA). However, your employer will have to withhold 20 percent for income taxes. To avoid the automatic withholding, you can withdraw money in smaller chunks. If you don't want to keep it in the employer's 401k when you leave the job, you can roll it over into a "rollover IRA," where it will then have to follow the rules of IRAs. If you have the money transferred directly to the financial institution where you will keep that IRA, there is no tax liability at that time.

One advantage of rollover IRAs is that if the money came from a 401k plan, it can go into another employer's 401k plan if you take another job. If you also have existing IRA accounts, the rollover should not be mixed with those.

Social Security Benefits

Social Security benefits don't arrive in your mail box automatically; you should apply about three months before you plan to retire, and you have some choices about exactly when that is. The government sets "full retirement" ages, ranging from 65 for people born in 1937 or earlier to 67 for those born in or after 1960. It also allows you to retire earlier, at age 62 in 2000, with reduced benefits. If you start receiving benefits at age 62, the amount is reduced permanently by 20 percent. If you choose an age somewhere between the earliest and your full-retirement point, benefits are permanently reduced by a smaller percentage. If you wait until age 70, the benefit increases by up to eight percent. Working doesn't prevent you from receiving benefits, although a portion of them may be taxable, depending on how much you earn.

How do you decide whether to wait and receive more or start collecting early? Find out what amounts you would receive in each scenario and see how many years it would take to make up for starting later, then decide.

How much can you expect? Not enough to live in a style you would like to become accustomed to. If you are married and both of you are eligible for benefits, you can choose between a married option or apply as two individuals; the government allows you to select the option that pays the most. Although the benefits are far from extravagant, they do increase over time, based on the Consumer Price Index.

Your benefit is based on what you paid in and how many years you worked, up to the maximum. You should receive an annual statement each year. If you don't, request one (see Resources at the end of the chapter).

Medicare Benefits and Misconceptions

If you have reached age 65 and are receiving Social Security benefits, you will receive Medicare automatically. Otherwise, you have to apply. In addition, you should purchase additional coverage, commonly referred to as "Medigap" insurance, which varies in price, depending on what's covered.

The most common misconception about Medicare is that it will cover nursing homes or assisted-living facilities — it doesn't, except for very brief stays immediately following hospitalization for an illness or injury. In later years, when care is needed, you're on your own unless you've purchased long term care (LTC) coverage. The cost of this varies dramatically, depending on your age and the benefits you select, and the best way to get a handle on the options is to sit down with a professional you trust. LTC coverage is discussed in more detail in the next chapter.

The Nitty Gritty

To select the right investment vehicles, you need to have a sense of your own future needs. There are many online sources to help you calculate your own financial scenario, and I've selected some of my favorites in the Resources section below. In a nutshell, the most critical questions to ask yourself are:

- How much income will I need to withdraw from my retirement savings (taking into account Social Security, pensions if any, and other income sources such as work)?
- When do I need to start withdrawing this income?
- When might I need more income and how much?

The answers to these questions aren't easy, and they will change as the years go by. However, if you give yourself at least a ten-year planning runway, your chances of success increase significantly.

resources

For information about bonds

The Bond Marketing Association www. investinginbonds.com

Wall Street Journal Interactive www.wsj.com

Full access to extensive bond and other investment information requires a subscription but the cost is reasonable.

For information about retirement issues

retireplan.about.com

www.seniors.gov

For Social Security and Medicare information www.ssa.gov

chapter 13

Estate Planning

Traditional estate planning has focused on determining what will happen to assets after an individual's death. However, more recent history has taught us that when people live longer, preserving sufficient wealth to live in dignity in later years is at least as important. Although longer life spans and medical miracles are wonderful things, they also bring new financial challenges that can sabotage the best intentions to leave something to one's heirs.

The sad fact is that expenses for long term care drive seven of ten senior families into poverty (below poverty levels defined by the federal government) within four months of a family member entering an institution for care, according to the National Council on Aging. Such care may require assistance with various aspects of normal daily living, due to physical or mental impairments, it may require some medical supervision, or a combination of both. Institutional care may be related to disease, or it may simply become necessary as a result of infirmity that develops as part of the aging process, with no medical services being needed.

Remarkable as it may seem, unrealistic expectations are one of the biggest reasons why so many seniors suffer this type of financial devastation. Too many people assume that Medicare or some other government program will pay for services whose costs must be borne by individuals.

Medicare and accompanying supplemental insurance plans

are strictly medical insurance. They only cover treatment of disease or injury and may cover limited extended care directly connected to an illness or injury. They don't cover costs of long term disability or age-related infirmity, yet nearly half of all Americans will most likely need some type of long term care at some time, according to the American Health Care Association.

Medicaid is the other government program people misunderstand. It doesn't provide coverage until an individual has spent their own assets to the point where he or she falls below the federal poverty threshold — which means all assets have effectively been spent.

To illustrate how financially devastating these misunderstandings can be: I recently met a widow in her eighties who relies on her children for support. She is in good spirits and good health, living an active life and working at a part-time job she enjoys. Before her husband died, he suffered from a debilitating disease for several years, requiring round-the-clock care not covered by any type of health insurance. In the process, their nest egg shrank from over $1.5 million (in 1980s dollars) to zero.

Is there a way to prevent these types of situations? Believe it or not, there is, with long term care insurance. And while it isn't the only aspect of estate planning that demands attention, we'll address it first because it seems to be the most widely misunderstood.

The Growing Need for Long Term Care

There are several factors that have created a need for long term care insurance, and longevity is one of them. In ancient Greece, the average lifespan was 18; for Puritans, the median was 33. Since then, our average lifespans have increased considerably, and they keep rising. Now, anyone who lives to age 65 is very likely to make it past 80 — well past 80 in the case of women — and the over-85 group is the fastest growing segment of the American population. This trend sets the stage for long term care needs.

Family members, about 72 percent of them women, provide about 80 percent of in-home long term care. This takes a significant toll. In one recent survey of women in caretaker roles, 41 percent had been forced to quit their job or take a leave of absence; half of these caretakers had to cut back on working hours and give up space in their home to accommodate the needs of their elderly loved one. According to the National Family Caregivers Association, 67 percent of adult children become depressed while taking care of their parents.

What are the options? Professional in-home care is certainly available, if funds are available to pay for it. But most people can't afford it, or can't afford as much of it as they would like, and the costs are rising significantly faster than inflation. Between 1995 and 2000, the average daily benefit offered by long term care insurance policies increased by 36 percent for in-home care and by 28 percent for nursing home care, according to the Health Insurance Association of America (HIAA).

Although most people prefer to stay out of an institution unless it's absolutely unavoidable, few are aware of the types of institutions that exist. They basically fall into two categories: those that provide assistance only with daily activities, such as eating, bathing, dressing, moving around and maintaining continence, and those that also offer skilled nursing care and have additional medical personnel on call as needed. As with any service or living facility, there is a range of quality in both categories, and as you might expect, having more funds means more options to choose from.

How Long Term Care Insurance Works

The most common question, "How much does it cost?" doesn't have a simple answer because the combination of benefits you buy can vary almost endlessly, and age is another critical factor. The low end of premiums is under $50 monthly, and the figure goes up to several hundred dollars or more. The HIAA found that the average annual premium in 2000 was $1,677. However, there is absolutely no way for you to get a sense of what you can get for how much unless you sit down with a qualified professional and look at your personal situation.

What do you get? Again, I have to stress the need for professional advice in making your choices of coverage, but these are some of the key elements of long term care benefits.

■ Type of coverage

The most basic type pays the costs of nursing home care only. It offers the lowest premium and the most bare bones coverage. If you want the policy to pay for in-home care, services in adult day care centers or assisted living facilities, it will cost more, but it will also provide more. Many people unwillingly end up in institutions because they can't afford anything else.

■ Daily benefit

Long term care policies pay a predetermined number of dollars for each day of care you receive. Naturally, the more your policy pays, the more options you have. Before making a decision, explore the types of care and costs in your area and in any other location you plan to live in later years.

■ Inflation protection

If you select this option, the dollar amount for your daily benefit will increase in proportion to the inflation rate. The rate increase can be calculated like simple or compound interest. The younger you are, the more important this option becomes.

■ Benefit period

There may be a time limit on how long you receive benefits after you start needing care, usually stated in years, or you can buy a lifetime plan that will pay for care as long as you live. Naturally, the latter costs more.

■ Elimination period

This is like a deductible, but instead of coverage kicking in after you pay a specified dollar amount, it kicks in after you've been receiving care for a stated number of days, which can be zero or 100 days or somewhere in between.

■ Nonforfeiture option

If you stop paying premiums, this option will give you some type of paid-up benefit, but it increases your premium.

The demand for care of all types will increase rapidly during the coming years. By 2030, more than 70 million people in this country will be age 65 or older — roughly twice the number at the beginning of the century — and those over age 85 are expected to total around nine million. Whether or not the growth in supply of services will be adequate to meet this demand remains to be seen, but it is certain that one's ability to pay for any type of service will be a critical factor in determining the quality of one's life. Long term care insurance can help to preserve both assets and personal dignity.

Inevitable Estate Planning Issues

No one likes to think about death, and few people like to make plans for a time when it will occur. As a result, about 70 percent of Americans die without a will, according to the American Bar Association. Devastating as the departure of a loved one may be, confusion surrounding their material affairs can compound the hardship, but it doesn't have to.

Although there are many books and software packages to help you create legal documents yourself, I feel that getting qualified legal advice is the most prudent way to do this. Even if you prefer the do-it-yourself approach, I suggest that you consult an estate planning attorney (see Resources for how to find a qualified one) to review your overall picture and make sure you've covered all the bases.

Following are some of the key issues every individual should include in their future planning.

- A will is the most basic element of estate planning, governing how assets will be distributed after your death. It also allows you to name an executor to make sure your wishes are followed. Regardless of any other estate planning tools you use, you need a will.

- Wills are subject to probate, a legal proceeding that courts use to make sure your will is valid and that debts are paid. The process is a matter of public record; it can take months or years and can be costly. A living trust, in conjunction with a will, can avoid probate. In essence, a living trust is a legal entity to which your assets are transferred during your lifetime. You, as the trustee, continue to control those assets until death, at which time your plan for distributing the assets goes into action. Whether or not you need a living trust depends on your personal circumstances and is definitely a matter that should be discussed with competent legal and financial professionals.

- Insurance policies, pension plans, various types of retirement plans and other financial instruments have beneficiaries you designated at some point. These should be reviewed periodically. Circumstances change, and so do the people to whom you want to leave your worldly possessions.

- Consider how you would want medical decisions to be made if you were incapacitated. You can designate a family member or friend to make medical decisions for you in such a situation by giving them a power of attorney for health care, or a health care proxy — what has been referred to as a "living will." Some states have declaration forms, available at hospitals, nursing homes and retirement centers, which you can fill in to make this designation.

- If you were incapacitated, how would you want financial decisions to be made for you? With a durable power of attorney you can select a relative or friend to act on your behalf. If you have a living trust, you may not need a durable power of attorney because you may already have designated that authority to a successor trustee.

- If you have children who need parental care, you need to name a guardian in the event of your death, or a court would have to make that decision. A guardian can be named in a will, along with a secondary choice in case the first named guardian is unable to care for your children. You can separate the duties of child care and management of your child's financial affairs among different guardians if you choose to.

- Your legal documents need to be kept in a secure place, and your loved ones need to know where they are.

What about Estate Taxes?

As I write this, they still exist. Although often believed to target primarily the richest Americans, estate tax statistics compiled by the National Center for Policy Analysis (NCPA) paint a different picture. In recent years, more than half of all estate taxes collected in America came from estates valued under $5 million. And if we look at what percentage of an estate is paid in taxes, in the real world, it's lower on estates valued over $20 million than on those valued between $5 and $20 million.

Recent history also shows that small family-owned businesses and farms experience the greatest hardships as a result of estate taxes. In the event of the principal owner's death, 51 percent of these small businesses would have significant difficulty surviving, and another 14 percent could not survive at all. One of the reasons for this is that while many of these businesses own substantial assets, they are not liquid, and when taxes must be paid, the law forces assets to be liquidated, incapacitating business operations.

While the NCPA found that only 2.03 percent of deaths in the United States are expected to result in estate taxes, those that are affected can be hit very hard. Savvy planning is the only way to avoid devastation as a result of these taxes, imposed by the federal government and by many states.

The first step in planning is to determine if your estate will owe taxes upon your death, and if so, how much, taking into account current federal and state laws. Making an inventory of assets may be a complex process, especially if you own a business. Even if you don't, there are pitfalls. I've met plenty of people whose insurance agent told them life insurance proceeds are "tax free." While this may be true in some cases, it certainly isn't in others.

As I said earlier, I am not a big believer in a do-it-yourself approach when it comes to estate planning because the stakes are just too high. So, rather than trying to tell you what to do (you already know I recommend getting professional advice), I'll offer some key issues for you to consider when it comes to estate taxes.

- Do you know what your estate consists of, its current value, and how much its value may increase in the future? Once you have a realistic estimate, you can determine if there will likely be an estate tax liability.
- Are you aware of how estate tax laws apply to your spouse, if you are married? Your plan should work regardless of which spouse outlives the other.

- If you have an estate tax liability, are there sufficient assets to cover these costs without unwanted liquidation? If not, a life insurance policy can be set up to fill the gap.

- Although living trusts are designed to bypass probate, not to impact estate taxes, there are other types of trusts that can help to minimize estate tax liability. If appropriate, the use of these should be considered.

When Gifts Exceed Their Face Value

Perhaps the simplest strategy for minimizing estate taxes when you die is to give gifts while you're still alive, up to the allowable annual maximum per person. Since both you and your spouse are allowed to give specified gift amounts per individual recipient without a gift tax liability, there are numerous possibilities to transfer a substantial amount of wealth without incurring penalties while you are living. For example, if you have two children and four grandchildren and you give each one $10,000 (or the maximum annual exclusion), that adds up to $60,000 in one year. If you include sons- or daughters-in-law, the total would be $80,000. Your spouse can give them an equal amount. There is no requirement that the recipient be a relative, so it could be anyone of your choice. The gift can be cash, investments or other assets, and the recipient owes no taxes as long as the value of each gift does not exceed allowable annual ceilings.

The Economic Growth and Tax Relief Reconciliation Act of 2001 set in motion a gradual phase-out of estate transfer taxes between 2002 and 2010. In the meantime, estate and gift tax rates vary, depending on the size of an estate. Where states levy estate taxes, those are in addition to federal amounts. Estate planning is a complex subject, so it pays to consult a professional and to plan ahead.

resources

American Health Care Association www.ahca.org

News about long term care and resources to help you make your own plans.

American College of Trust and Estate Counsel www.actec.org

In addition to technical information designed primarily for professionals, the site enables consumers to locate estate planning attorneys and links to information sources geared to consumers.

chapter 14

Family Matters

It seems that most families have an unwritten rule when it comes to money: Don't talk about it, at least not in a sane, rational manner that involves any significant degree of planning. Like sex, money can be a very volatile subject. But while discussion of sexual topics has become much more acceptable in recent years, money remains in the closet.

You may think I'm exaggerating. We can get financial news around the clock on television, on our computers and even on our wireless phones, anywhere in the world. Maybe your co-workers join forces to buy lottery tickets and talk about how they would spend the money if they won. So where's the lack of communications about money?

None of this noisy chatter deals with real life — how you and your family live today, tomorrow and twenty or thirty years from now. Can you afford that vacation you're planning? Are you over-spending on holiday gifts? How will your kids' college tuition be paid? Is there any equity left in your home? Are you working much longer hours than you'd like, just to make payments on a car that's at least as much status symbol as transportation?

If you regularly discuss your income, spending, saving and investment plans with your spouse, you feel confident that your kids will grow up financially sensible and secure, you're all set for your own retirement and you have no concerns about how your aging parents will be taken care of if they need help, congratulations! You're in a small, "lucky" (due to your own diligence) minority. In that case, reading on will be enlightening as to the planning the rest of America has to come to grips with.

The Biggest Hurdle

Lack of communication about money is the most basic financial problem families face. Before looking at raising financially savvy children or taking care of aging parents, let's pause to consider a common dilemma for couples — talking about money. The Consumer Credit Counseling Service of Los Angeles offers many low-cost or no-cost educational seminars on financial topics, but none for couples. Its couples program was cancelled because arguments between spouses became so heated that none of the instructors was willing to put up with the brouhaha. None of its other programs has experienced a similar problem.

Many of my clients are couples. Since I would seldom meet with one spouse without the other present, I am quite familiar with the recurring issues that cause problems. Simply not talking about financial goals and priorities is the biggest error couples make. I can't speculate why this dialogue is so often absent, and I don't know of anyone who claims to understand why the silence exists, but I and every other financial professional I know observes the same phenomenon. Because discussion has never taken place, when it does, there is so much uncommunicated, bottled-up "stuff" that it's very easy for the conversation to take on volcanic qualities.

However, I still see a glass half full. If there is some understanding of the key areas that need to be discussed, along with a genuine desire to create a decent financial future, two people who have an otherwise desirable relationship can learn to plan and manage their finances reasonably well. Below are some of the critical issues that must be addressed. Some common ground has to be established on each point — enough to formulate and put a plan into practice.

■ Set a time to discuss finances and be prepared

Although it isn't exactly a romantic date with your "other half," this type of discussion requires your and your partner's full attention. It shouldn't take place randomly, when one of you is tired, or at a time usually slated for a favorite activity. You should be prepared for a rational discussion, just as you would prepare for a business meeting, and you should make this "date" on a regular basis to keep tabs on changing needs and progress. Perhaps most important: You should both be prepared to treat the other with respect and not to assign blame or fault for whatever may be wrong with your financial picture.

■ Review your income, spending and debt figures together

You should both be aware of what's coming in, what's going out and where that leaves you. If you don't like what you see, realize that you share the responsibility for letting it get that way, even if only by ignoring history while it was being written.

■ Talk about your overall goals and how your finances relate

Many people never discuss the future beyond where they will vacation or who they're inviting over for dinner. Try talking about your individual and mutual long-term goals and what's realistic to accomplish over a period of a few months, a few years, ten years, twenty ... whatever time frame is comfortable. Look further into the future as you get more comfortable with this approach. Set one or more tangible, attainable objectives that will take you toward broader goals — something like putting $10 a week in a savings account or paying off a credit card and locking it in a drawer. Write these down so that you can track what you've accomplished.

■ See if you have dramatically different financial "personalities"

Sometimes one person is a habitual saver while the other is a spender; or one likes to take risks when investing and the other is extremely conservative; sometimes the differences are more subtle. If your financial attitudes are like oil and water, come to some compromises or work out a way to temper each other's extremes. The key is to find a point on which you agree and build on that foundation.

■ **Learn to be creative in solving problems**

Few people have more money than they know what to do with. Doing the most with what you have takes patience and practice, but it can be extremely rewarding and may result in you having more wealth than you expected in the future. For example, if you see that you're dining out more than you should — financially speaking — maybe improving your culinary skills and cooking great meals at home can help to pay off a credit card.

Learning To Think Wealthy

Learning how the rich think is a good starting point for building your own path to a family fortune. But I'd like to stress that the type of mentality I'm talking about here is not some form of "positive thinking" that is supposed to make money magically materialize in your lap. Although a positive attitude is certainly productive — necessary, in fact — in and of itself it won't do the trick.

In the real world, "thinking rich" boils down to a mindset that is predominant among self-made, financially successful people. This mindset is really a set of values that defines priorities in managing money and governs both day-to-day financial habits and bigger-picture decisions involving money.

Interestingly enough, my observations of wealthy people pretty closely match those of other professionals who have studied how self-made millionaires and billionaires got to be that way. These are some of the key traits that distinguish wealth accumulators from the rest of the population.

- They are aware of how their actions today will impact their future. In other words, they see a clear connection between how they deal with money day-to-day and their financial situation down the road.
- They have the discipline to make plans and carry them out, both in regards to money and other aspects of life.
- They are frugal, generally spending less than they can afford.
- They work hard in their chosen field.
- They create and maintain a stable home environment.
- They measure success in relation to their own goals, not by how large their house is or how new their car is.
- They don't have a habit of impulse buying.
- They do not seek to acquire status by buying symbols of success that they can't afford.
- They are motivated by something other than a desire to spend.
- Those who generate the most wealth also tend to have a vision that is a little ahead of their time, or at least different from the majority. (However, vision alone doesn't guarantee financial success.)

In the case of couples, sharing some of the above perspectives makes life a lot easier and sets the stage for greater success financially.

Teaching Kids about Money

Although the wisest parents can't always raise a financially smart child, the odds are against you if you don't make an effort. And the most basic element is the example you set. "Do as I say, not as I do," won't work.

The toy industry is forever inventing new toys that claim to teach children many things, including finance. So much so that parents who continually live above their means could run up even higher credit card bills by buying the "latest and greatest" to try and turn Junior into the financial genius they know they'll never be. Sadly, it won't work. Even if Junior rebels and becomes a penny pincher, he or she might become so obsessive about saving that life is a misery. Either way, the story doesn't have a happy ending.

For many people, setting a good example is the most difficult way to educate their children, but that doesn't change how things work. And if you know your financial habits need improvement, maybe the well-being of your child will provide the extra incentive you need to make a change for the better.

With that in mind, there are specific things parents can do to educate their kids about money. The most basic lesson has to do with consequences — learning that they exist in the world of money. Giving a child an allowance is a starting point. How much, how early depends on your child's ability to grasp numbers and concepts, and only you can judge that. Experts' opinions vary on those points and on whether there should be strings attached. For example, should the allowance be contingent upon the child doing chores or keeping his or her bedroom tidy? There is no single answer, so you have to decide which way to go and at what ages.

To teach children that money can grow, both parents and classrooms have had great success by setting up an imaginary bank, even with very young children. In these scenarios, the children are given an allowance along with the choice of leaving it in the "bank" to earn a specified amount of interest or spending it. It may surprise you that children (more so than adults) often prefer to earn interest rather than spend. The key is to make the concept understandable before they make the decision. In addition, many banks today offer accounts for children.

Another issue children need to learn is the connection between work and money — it doesn't just come out of ATM machines. Kids will get it if parents explain that their work results in the dollars they bring home and that the government also takes a share. Again, how you explain and in what degree of detail, at what age, is up to your best judgment.

Other things you can do include opening a small investment account and letting your child see how the money is growing and/or giving him or her the option of investing some of the allowance. Involving children in financial decisions for the family is also good education. And encouraging children to get some type of paid work, be it baby sitting or walking the neighbor's dog, once they're old enough, definitely gets across the idea of working to earn money.

And don't forget: You learned about money somehow, whether it was a good education or not. Things that worked for you as a kid might work for yours. And if your experience wasn't so good, maybe it can be a springboard for better ways to orient your offspring to the dollars and cents of life.

Talking to Parents

It seems that once kids are grown up, their parents still have a hard time talking to them about money, and as parents age, living alone, or not, becomes the most critical issue that stays under the table. A recent survey for AARP found that about two-thirds of both baby boomers and their parents have not discussed issues relating to the parents' living independently or not in the future. Strangely enough, both groups also feel that it would be easy or very easy to discuss these issues. So why haven't they?

The same survey also found conflicting views about how much boomers help their aging parents. The kids say they help more than the parents think they do — but maybe that's not exactly news for these two generations.

Another finding: Both the parents and the kids would prefer that the parents live independently for as long as possible, and neither group wants anyone to end up in a nursing home if it's at all avoidable. However, neither generation seems to want to start talking to each other, and neither one has as much information about living alternatives as they would like.

Yet other research, by the Phoenix Home Life Mutual Insurance Company, found that about 40 percent of adults age thirty to sixty already provide or expect to provide financial support to aging parents. This figure is up from 22 percent in 1994. Again, why aren't these parents and children talking about this with each other?

While I don't know why, I can appreciate how difficult it is because of my own experiences. No one claims to have the ultimate solution for this communication gap. But if each of us recognizes that the gap is there and that it makes life more difficult for all concerned, perhaps more of us will start talking.

Luckily, there is plenty of information available about living alternatives and to support family caregivers. Often, knowing more about the options can make the subject easier to broach, and the options are continually expanding as more and more people live longer. There are different types of in-home help, depending on individual needs; there are centers offering activities and care for older adults during the day (adult day-care centers); and there are various levels of care available in different living facilities. In addition, there is help for family caregivers.

If you want to enlist the help of a professional to determine what options exist for an elderly person, there are geriatric care managers. These individuals are trained and certified to be able to assess an elderly person's ability to take care of himself or herself and to see what all the options are if help is needed. To find out more about how care managers work and how to locate such a professional in your area, contact the National Association of Professional Geriatric Care Managers (see Resources). There are fees involved, but they are very reasonable considering the knowledge these people can put to work for you.

In the future, it is likely that more and more government-funded help will be available, especially for family caregivers. One easy way to find out about what's going on in this area is through the Administration on Aging, a federal agency (see Resources). But no matter how many new programs are developed, adult children and parents discussing future options is the first step. If you are stuck and work with a financial advisor, enlist his or her help.

resources

Administration on Aging www.aoa.gov

AARP www.aarp.org
www.mygeneration.org

National Association of Professional Geriatric Care Managers
www.caremanager.org

chapter 15

Getting the Right Financial Advice

Most people I meet started learning about financial planning in the same way they found out about the "birds and the bees." But while nature forces us to gain a working knowledge of our bodies sooner or later, there is no "natural" way for human beings to become innately aware of how money really works. Consequently, many people rely on financial advice from others who are no more, and sometimes less, financially savvy.

A survey by the Opinion Research Corporation International, based in Princeton, NJ, found that 86 percent of people who make investments rely on others for advice when selecting financial products and services. The study, which polled a nationally representative sample of 1,000 adults, found that more people (68 percent) seek advice from family and friends than from professionals (51 percent).

How much of a difference does professional advice make? A study by the Financial Planning Association found that 85 percent of people who use a professional financial advisor are extremely or very satisfied, especially in terms of having greater peace of mind, a clear sense of financial direction, and being closer to realizing their financial and life goals. The level of satisfaction is even higher — 91 percent — among those using a Certified Financial Planner (CFP), a professional whose designation I'll address in more detail in a moment.

How does the Internet figure into the picture? It certainly enables floods of information to flow onto your desktop, but that doesn't necessarily simplify financial decision making. Exceptional markets in the late 1990s encouraged many otherwise shy investors to venture into online brokerages in droves. However, when stocks dipped significantly in 2000, a sad fact emerged: a booming market had given relatively inexperienced investors a false sense of financial acumen. And when the chips dove down, use of online-only brokerages followed, decreasing much more dramatically than use of brokerages that also offer services through traditional channels with real live person-to-person contact. The biggest drop in online visitors, by nearly one third, was among those earning more than $100,000 per year, according to a survey by Jupiter Media Metrix. The same survey found that the higher-net-worth online investors also use traditional investment advisors.

During the same spate of poor market performance, another study, by Gomez, Inc., based in Waltham, MA, found that online investors shifted their focus from shorter-term gains to longer-term goals. Just prior to the downturn, approximately 41 percent considered themselves life goal planners, but shortly after, over 56 percent took on a longer-term, life goal perspective.

In my experience (and that of every other financial planner I know), volatile markets cause people to question their choices. If there's a big upswing in a sector of stocks, such as in technology in the latter part of the 1990s, the most common question is "do I own enough?" The feeling of maybe missing out on huge gains can cause a lot of stress, so much so that many people get the urge to throw a good plan out the window in a frenzy to get rich quick. Unfortunately, the results can be tragic. And in down markets, fear drives investors to sell at huge losses. In both situations, a trained professional with an objective view and a real understanding of a client's goals can help to avert financial disasters and maintain peace of mind.

To Do It Yourself or Not

There is a certain — be it small — percentage of the population that excels at making financial plans and following through with them. If you are a member of that select group, I salute you and hope you pass on the wisdom to your children and as many other people as possible. For the rest of the world, a do-it-yourself approach presents a few pitfalls, unrealistic expectations being one.

Opinion Research Corporation International conducted "Great Expectations" surveys on 1,000 adults that are representative of the general population. They found that those with the lowest incomes expected some of the highest returns. Among people earning less than $15,000 annually, 13 percent expected returns of more than 40 percent per year, compared to only 5 percent of total respondents being as optimistic (or should I say, unrealistic). Historically, the U.S. equity market return has averaged around 10 percent annually.

You may be thinking, so what if some people's expectations are high, they'll find out eventually. Not so. Expectations and emotions drive investment decisions, especially irrational ones. If you expect to earn 40 percent in the coming year, and six months from now you've only earned 3 percent, or even seen a decline, the "logical" conclusion is that you've invested in the wrong place — so you sell and buy something else, perhaps with slightly less principal. The next investment also doesn't seem to work, and even though your money has shrunk some more, you're sure you just made another mistake in your choice of mutual fund, for example. So you sell again at a loss and try again and again and again. Even worse, you might hear a "hot stock tip" and act on it, suffering an even bigger loss.

If this sounds far fetched, consider some actual numbers. Between January 1984 and December 1998, the S&P 500 index returned an average of 17.9 percent per year. According to a study by Dalbar, Inc., the typical investor earned only 7.25 percent during those 15 years because of attempts to time the market. Those who followed a buy-and-hold strategy earned more. During the same 15 years, the S&P 500 returned more than ten times its initial value, while the average investor's growth was less than three times the initial sum.

Planning with the Pros

There are three key factors that distinguish more affluent investors from their poorer counterparts: experience, discipline and focusing on longer-term goals. If you're just starting to invest, you can make up for lack of personal experience by learning from experienced professionals. The other two factors are personal choices, regardless of your age or history. In addition, if you have an advisor that is right for you, that person can help to keep you on your own path — something that is becoming more and more difficult in a culture where we are bombarded with financial information and opinions around the clock.

Aside from the question of whether to work with a professional, there is the matter of what type. The term "financial planning" is not regulated. Unlike legal or medical services, which can only be provided by licensed practitioners, financial planning services can be offered by virtually anyone. The National Association of Securities Dealers licenses and regulates individuals selling securities, such as stock brokers and registered investment advisors, but not "financial planners" or the process of "financial planning." Consequently, insurance agents, stock brokers, accountants and even attorneys sometimes offer financial planning services. In practice, the term is often used to market specific financial products because it sounds more appealing than "come and hear my sales pitch."

In all fairness, some of the individuals in those professions do have your best interests at heart when they hang out a financial-planning shingle, but there is such a thing as a pro who specializes in and has a credential in financial planning: a Certified Financial Planner, or CFP. That term is trademarked and regulated by the Certified Financial Planner Board of Standards, in Denver, CO, and anyone representing themselves as a CFP must be licensed by the board to use the designation. Here's what the CFP board requires before it lets you use those letters after your name: at least three years of related experience along with adequate education; passing of a certification exam; adherence to the board's code of ethics; and the meeting of specified continuing education requirements. In addition, the board has the power to suspend or revoke a license if its standards are not upheld.

What is financial planning? According to the Financial Planning Association (FPA), in Washington, DC, the membership organization for CFPs, it's "the process of wisely managing your finances so that you can achieve your dreams and goals — while at the same time helping you negotiate the financial barriers that inevitably arise in every stage of life." The FPA offers consumers a more extensive explanation, tips on selecting a financial planner and a list of at least three CFPs in your local area (see Resources). In addition, you can find out if the CFP Board of Standards has taken any disciplinary action against a planner by contacting the board directly.

The financial planning process starts with a discussion of your goals and your current situation and the formulation of a personal plan. However, that's just the tip of the iceberg. The most important aspect of a relationship between you and a financial planner is the management of your resources in a way that achieves your personal goals. That's an ongoing process that requires continual vigilance and communication, with discussion about decisions you face over the years and solutions to problems that arise.

The biggest challenge is to keep your goals in sight and stick with your plan. The times when my clients need me most is when new obstacles arise in life or when markets dip. Interestingly enough, my job then isn't to come up with new strategies but to review what the client's goals are (they're easy to forget) and why the planned strategy will attain those goals.

Selecting the Right Person

In essence, working with a financial planner is a partnership, one that should last some years. So it makes sense to examine your options. To learn about planners in your area, in addition to contacting the FPA, ask family and friends if they work with a planner. I don't recommend choosing a professional just because your best friend is happy with that individual, but it makes sense to include them on your initial list. Then do your research, which should include meeting with the people who look most likely, and make your own choice.

The criteria you use in your selection process, I believe, falls into two separate areas: technical skills, experience and credentials — hard facts, so to speak — and the human factor — does the chemistry work for you personally? The latter is impossible to quantify, but below are some questions you can ask yourself after meeting with planners.

- Did they treat me with respect?
- Did they ask about my concerns, then pay close attention to those needs?
- Did they explain things simply and to my satisfaction?
- Did they talk to me as an equal, as opposed to talking down to me?

- Was I encouraged to call with questions?
- Was I allowed time to make a decision as opposed to being pushed into one?
- Will they let me retain control, as opposed to wanting me to sign it over? When you hear those horror stories of advisors ripping people off, it's usually because the client has signed over control. Never do that.
- Were they willing to give me references?

On the more tangible side, it's important to know the strengths and limitations of a prospective planner. There is a trend today toward specialization, and sometimes it goes too far. Retirement planning is one area where this can happen with "retirement specialists." It seems that the financial services world offers more products with the word "retirement" attached than any other buzzword, giving impetus to all sorts of new marketing approaches that may distract you from getting real financial help.

While there is nothing wrong with an emphasis on retirement planning, if that is your primary goal, working with a "retirement specialist" may be prone to some distinct pitfalls. You don't save for retirement in a vacuum — life goes on with its constant financial challenges. If those aren't addressed objectively as part of an overall plan, you may not get maximum mileage out of your dollars. Another possible pitfall is that the planning will focus on investments apparently designed just for retirement. In actual fact, whether or not an investment vehicle is suitable for retirement depends on how you use it and your personal situation.

Let's say you just inherited enough money to buy the car of your dreams, pay off a significant chunk of your mortgage or make a significant investment in your golden years. Someone sits in front of you showing you how that money will turn to millions if you invest it all now in the mutual funds they represent. The sales pitch becomes background noise as you envision driving along a beautiful coastal road in your new car. Then, as the number crunching invades the salty air, you start to feel guilty about wanting to enjoy life.

This isn't what I mean by "financial planning." If you know you should be planning for your future and genuinely want to do so, you deserve some respect and objective advice from a qualified professional who cares about your goals. With that in mind, these are some questions to ask in seeking the financial planner that's right for you.

- What credentials and licenses do you hold?
- What organizations are you affiliated with?
- What is your education and experience?
- Do you have minimum net worth, income or asset requirements?
- What types of clients do you typically work with?
- Over what time period do you generally work with clients?
- Do you specialize in dealing with any particular type of situation?
- What services do you provide?
- How would you work with me (e.g., scheduled meetings, contact by phone or email, your availability if a new situation arises)?
- Would anyone else work with me on your behalf?
- What do you look for in a client?
- What relationships do you have with other companies or professionals, e.g., with companies whose products you sell or with professionals who provide related services?
- How do you get paid?

The important things to keep in mind are that any questions you personally have should be answered to your satisfaction. If they aren't, keep looking. Or, if you just don't feel comfortable with the person, that individual isn't right for you.

Financial planning is a very personal thing. You will have to disclose a lot of financial information and to discuss personal situations. When considering a professional, ask yourself if you would feel comfortable addressing the financial aspects of these types of issues with that person:

- plans for getting married or divorced
- plans for having or adopting a child
- saving for retirement
- paying for a child's college education
- taking care of an aging parent
- buying or selling a house
- buying or leasing a car
- spending a significant sum on a special vacation
- investing in a business or rental real estate
- dealing with a financial crisis
- dealing with a relative's financial crisis
- the financial aspects of a death in the family
- dealing with a windfall, such as an inheritance.

Financial Planning Fees

Over the years, financial planners have been compensated in a number of ways, including fee-only, commission, or a combination of fee and commission. The types of fees vary, and it's important to understand the differences.

"Fee-only" has been used to describe a fixed fee for a service, for example, a flat fee for drawing up a financial plan. In practice, this type of compensation is being used less frequently by itself. More likely, you may find planners charging a combination of set fees and commissions. And asset-based management fees are being used more often. These types of fees are a percentage of the total value of assets a planner is managing. For example, if the total value is $250,000 and the management fee is one percent annually, it would be $2,500 per year. In the following year, if the value of assets grew to $275,000, the annual management fee, still one percent, would be $2,750. A planner may or may not receive commissions in addition to management fees. The most important thing is for you to understand how a given planner is compensated and to decide for yourself if that seems right for you.

The Overriding Factor

You are the one who sets your goals and ultimately determines your financial future. And you are the only person who can judge whether a professional is the right one for you — or if you even want to get professional advice. Whether you work alone or enlist the services of a professional financial planner, I hope that you have clear goals in sight and execute a practical plan to achieve them.

resources

Financial Planning Association www.fpanet.org
The site offers a search tool to locate Certified Financial Planners in your area.

Certified Financial Planner Board of Standards www.cfp-board.org
The Board can verify a Certified Financial Planner's credentials and track record.

chapter 16

Answers to Ten Important Questions

As you make plans and work to bring them to fruition, various questions will arise. It's important to get these answered, to enhance your knowledge and to make sure that you have adequate information before making decisions.

1 | What are Class A, B and C shares?

Although commissions sound pretty self-explanatory — you buy mutual funds and pay a sales commission, for example — they can work in different ways. When you invest in a mutual fund, you are buying shares in that fund. But there may be three classes of shares — Class A, B and C — each with a different commission structure.

Before looking at how each type of share works, it's important to understand that all mutual funds (including no-load ones) have an "expense ratio," expressed as a percentage of money you have invested in the fund. The expense ratio is the total of the annual expenses of the fund, aside from any sales charge at the time shares are purchased or redeemed, and it is paid annually by shareholders as a percentage of their investment. Every fund prospectus shows what expense percentage it charges annually. The expense ratio differs for different classes of mutual fund shares, as do sales charges.

Class A shares charge a front-end sales charge: a percentage of your money is deducted off the top. For example, if a fund's front-end sales charge is 3 percent and you invest $1,000, $30 will be deducted and $970 will be placed in your fund account to grow over time. When you sell your shares, there is no fee — you get the total of the value of your account at that time. The expense ratio for Class A shares will be lower than those for the other classes. Some funds offer discounts on front-end sales charges if you invest more than a specified amount. For example, with an investment of up to $50,000 the sales charge may be 5 percent, but on investment amounts between $50,000 and $100,000 the fee may be reduced to 4.75 percent, with even lower fees on larger investments.

Class B shares have a contingent deferred sales charge (CDSC). If you invest $1,000, the whole amount goes into your fund account to grow. However, when you sell your shares, a sales charge may be deducted at that time, depending on how long your money remained in the fund. Typically, the CDSC declines with every year you own the shares, down to zero after a preset number of years, often seven years. If you hold the shares until the CDSC is eliminated, you never pay a sales load. The expense ratio for Class B shares will be higher. However, Class B shares may "convert" to Class A shares once the CDSC is eliminated, and would then charge a lower expense ratio, comparable to that of Class A shares.

Class C shares generally don't charge any up-front sales charge but may charge a redemption fee if you sell shares in a short time, usually within a year. Their expense ratio will be higher than that of Class A and B shares.

Which class of share is better for you depends on your situation, such as your goals for a given sum of money and the time frame you have to reach those objectives.

2 | What is the best way to save for college?

As with all financial planning, the length of time you have, your needs and resources determine what's best for you, but these are some of the key things to keep in mind.

As a general rule, the more you save, either in your own name or in your child's, the less likely you are to receive financial aid. (While this may seem discouraging, keep in mind that earning an income also disqualifies you from receiving welfare — not a bad thing.) A great deal of financial aid comes in the form of loans to your child, which can add up a hefty debt after graduation, so it's better to avoid this path if possible.

While any college savings are better than none, those that minimize tax liabilities are best. If you have a decade or two to amass tuition fees and other college costs, consider state-sponsored savings plans under Section 529 of the Internal Revenue Code. The exact rules governing these vary from one state to another, but there are some underlying principles across the board.

Contributions to 529 plans are not tax deductible, but the money grows without being taxed each year, similar to IRA or 401k funds. The account is established in the child's name, but the donor controls the funds until the child starts post-secondary education. Contributions can be made by parents, grandparents and even aunts and uncles. There is no estate or gift tax liability if the contribution doesn't exceed $50,000 per contributor ($100,000 for a married couple) for a five-year period and there are no other gifts to that child within that time period. Most states set a lifetime contribution maximum, but it is generous and increases as college costs rise.

These plans are also flexible in other ways. There are no income ceilings for the donor, and there are no age limits for the child. The college can be anywhere in the United States, can be private, public, graduate or vocational school, as long as it is an accredited post-secondary institution. If the child decides not to go to college, the funds can be transferred to another family member. The funds are taxable at the child's rate when withdrawn for tuition, and some states forego state taxes.

What if the child never goes to college? If disability or death is the reason, the donor can withdraw the funds without any penalty, paying regular income taxes on the earned portion. There are also no penalties if the child receives a scholarship. Otherwise, the donor pays a 10-percent penalty on earnings, as well as regular income taxes (on the earnings portion only).

As you might expect, there is a down side: investment options may be somewhat limited. However, there is a trend of investment choices multiplying. A good way to get more specific information about an individual state's plan is through the College Savings Plans Network, www.collegesavings.org, an organization affiliated with the National Association of State Treasurers. The Web site offers links to just about everything you would ever want to know about paying for college, including extensive information about financial aid and scholarships.

3 | Are Section 529 plans the same as prepaid tuition plans?

No, the two are different plans. Prepaid tuition plans are usually set up for the child to attend a specific college, generally in your state of residence. Therefore, they put limits on your child's options. In addition, the investment options may be less attractive with prepaid plans. While it's not a good idea to reject any option across the board, I recommend that you learn about all your choices and get some professional financial planning advice before you opt for a prepaid tuition plan.

4 | What about Education IRAs?

These are another option, but you can't use this method along with Section 529 plans or state prepaid tuition plans, or if you earn over a specified amount, which is adjusted each year. Education IRAs may also disqualify your child from receiving certain federal education grants or scholarships. You can save up to $2,000 per year per child in these IRAs. The contribution is not tax deductible, but savings grow on a tax-deferred basis. When the money is withdrawn for primary, secondary or higher education, it is tax free. As with prepaid tuition plans, I recommend that you get some professional financial planning advice before choosing this path.

5 | How can I pay for college if I didn't save and my teenager is almost ready to graduate from high school?

First, see how you can keep the costs as low as possible. Explore local two-year community colleges that offer credits that are transferable to four-year programs in universities. The tuition will be a fraction of what you would pay otherwise for the first two years. That, combined with having your teenager live at home during college years, can save as much as 60 percent on the total college costs. At the same time, find out about every type of available financial aid and apply as soon as possible.

Another option is to tap into a home equity line of credit. You can generally borrow up to 80 percent of the equity in your home, and interest may be tax deductible. And you don't have to spend any of your credit until bills come due, be they tuition bills or other college costs.

If you're considering liquidating any investments, look at growth stocks you've held for some time. Long-term capital gains tax should set you back significantly less than taxes on other types of earnings.

6 We would like to give our daughter and her husband a sizable loan so that they can buy a home. How should we set this up?

You should do it much like any other lender would, with an attorney drawing up a mortgage agreement that gives you a lien on your daughter's new home. When it comes to interest, the IRS has some specific rules for situations such as yours where the loan exceeds $10,000.

If you charge a market rate of interest, your daughter will be able to deduct the interest payments from her income, just as she would with any home mortgage, and you will pay taxes on the income you receive. However, if you choose to charge a lower rate of interest, or no interest at all, things become a little more complicated. The IRS will allow your child to take a deduction as though she was paying full market interest. At the same time, you will have to pay taxes as though you were receiving the market rate — even though you aren't actually receiving the money.

To illustrate, here's an example. Suppose you lend your daughter $150,000 at 5-percent interest when the market rate is 9 percent. She pays you $7,500 a year in interest instead of a fair market amount of $13,500. Under the IRS rules, you still have to pay income tax on the full $13,500 and your child can deduct all $13,500 even though she didn't pay all of it.

This situation raises another important issue: a potential gift tax liability. The IRS considers the $6,000 difference ($13,500 market value interest minus actual interest of $7,500) as a gift from you to your child subject to gift tax rules. As long as that amount, combined with any other gifts to your child that year, remains below the annual gift tax exclusion, you won't have to pay gift taxes. Otherwise, you will.

In addition, before making such a loan, establish the required pay-back interest rate and schedule so that the benefits you provide your daughter do not negatively impact your own personal financial plan.

7 | What's the best way to pay down my mortgage?

If you're serious about eliminating your mortgage debt ahead of schedule, the key is to have a clear strategy and follow it. If you decide to put "extra money" towards the mortgage in a haphazard way, it will probably never happen. These are four possible strategies.

■ Pay a fixed extra amount each month

Add a specific number of dollars to your regular payment each month. For example, if you pay $25 extra each month on a 30-year, 9-percent, $100,000 mortgage, you'll repay the loan about four years early and save almost $30,000. If you pay $100 extra each month instead of $25, you'll shave off more than 10 years and save over $75,000.

You can start making those extra payments at any time during the loan. However, you should notify your lender that the additional amounts should go toward principal and keep track of the prepayments to double-check them against the lender's records. Verifying that your payments are correctly credited is vital because lending institutions do sometimes make mistakes.

■ Refinance

This strategy works if your interest rate is significantly higher than current rates and you still have a number of years left on your mortgage. For example, suppose you have 18 years left on a 30-year, 11-percent, $100,000 mortgage. If you refinance the outstanding balance (about $90,000) with a 15-year, 8-percent loan, you'll save about $14,000 after expenses (closing costs). The loan will be paid near the original pay-off date. It makes sense if you're planning to live in your current home long enough to recover closing costs.

■ Make biweekly payments

Instead of making your scheduled monthly payment, pay half that amount every two weeks. By doing this, you will be paying the equivalent of 13 monthly payments each year. If you keep it up, your 30-year mortgage will be paid in 20 years. How much you save depends on the total borrowed, when you start making the biweekly payments and the interest rate, but the savings could be about as much as your original loan.

Some lenders don't accept biweekly payments. If yours is one of these, here's how you can achieve the same result: Divide the principal and interest portion of your monthly mortgage payment by 12 and add this amount to each payment. Make sure the extra dollars are credited toward principal.

■ Earmark expected extra income

This approach works if you regularly receive bonuses at year end, periodic commission earnings on top of a regular salary or do some type of work outside your normal job. The key is to commit the money from that source to your mortgage before you get the check, then pay that amount as soon as it comes in. Again, keep records and make sure these amounts are correctly credited to your mortgage principal.

8 | How should I determine what type of mortgage is best for me: 15- or 30-year, fixed or adjustable rate?

Shorter mortgage terms mean higher payments. In practice, that means you can buy less house with the same income. Lenders use a formula to determine the size of mortgage you qualify for, based predominantly on the required monthly payment, your verifiable income and other financial obligations. (Mortgages that require less or no documentation of income require higher down payments and/or higher interest rates.) If you're more frugal than the average person or realistically expect your income to increase significantly in the near term, you won't score extra points. Consequently, a 15-year mortgage will limit your home-buying options. With a 30-year mortgage, you have the option of prepaying and can equal or even exceed the benefits of a 15-year term.

When choosing a fixed or adjustable-rate loan, the key question to answer is: How long will you live in this home? If you plan to move within a few years, the adjustable option should offer a lower rate of interest. For peace of mind, you can get loans where the first few years are fixed and beyond that, there is a ceiling on how high the interest rate can go. If, on the other hand, you expect to stay put for a long time, the fixed rate generally makes more sense.

9 | Recently, my mother passed away, and I had no idea where her will was or what I should do. I don't want my children to face the same problem. What can I do?

As you learned, it is imperative for your family to know where your will is kept, but there is another type of document that is often overlooked but equally important: a letter of instruction. This informal document can be difficult to write but will make things much easier for those you care about. It can cover the key issues you had to deal with, including a list of things you want done, such as notifying family members, friends, an employer, an insurance company and details about other personal wishes that are not likely to be covered as precisely in a will.

Other information that a letter of instruction may convey includes: wishes for burial arrangements; any organ donation requests; a list of assets; a list of advisors such as financial planners, stock brokers, insurance agents, accountants and attorneys, with contact information; and personal messages to survivors.

A letter of instruction is not legally binding in most states, as a will is, but it can cover many details that would otherwise be left to chance. And it can be updated by you without incurring the time and expense of an attorney. A copy of it should be kept with your will, your attorney should have a copy and you should keep another copy in your home.

10 | I live with someone I love very much, but we do not plan to get married. I would like my partner to inherit everything I own. Are there any estate planning pitfalls I should be aware of?

If an individual dies without a will, state intestacy laws will determine who receives assets — generally blood relatives — so a will is mandatory. However, even a will may not guarantee that your wishes will be carried out if disinherited relatives challenge your directives. To prevent this from happening, the will should include an explanation of why any family members were not given an inheritance. In addition, it is very important for your partner not to be a witness when your will is drafted.

Other documents, such as durable powers of attorney and health care proxies, may also be questioned unless you attach a letter explaining why you chose to give legal authority to your partner rather than a relative.

A revocable trust, with you as the trustee during your lifetime and your partner succeeding you as trustee upon your death, avoids the time delays and costs of probate. In addition, a trust, unlike a will, is not a matter of public record. However, an explanation of why you assigned trusteeship to your partner rather than a relative should be part of the trust document because relatives can challenge your partner's trusteeship just as they can challenge a will.

While there are more and more people in your situation, attitudes and laws are not necessarily keeping pace. As a result, it is critical that you work with an experienced estate planning attorney to draw up all the documents. While competent legal counsel is important in all estate planning, it merits special attention in this type of relationship. By understanding the potential pitfalls and dealing with them in your planning, there is no reason why your wishes can't be carried out.

chapter 17

Remembering the Basics

I started writing this book during an economic boom. Before the book was completed, the economy began a downward slide, and America engaged in a war against terrorism. Fortunately, I didn't have to go back to square one and rewrite everything because, regardless of how heartening or depressing economic swings may seem, the basics of sound financial management don't change. It may be difficult to believe that fact at times, but it's true.

Communications technology poses one of the biggest challenges to financial sanity because it is a double-edged sword. On the one hand, technology has enabled almost anyone in this country to access vast amounts of financial information and trade like a pro; on the other, it has condensed the time it takes for information to travel, to such an extent that a market fluctuation in a far corner of the world can dramatically influence the balance of your nest egg more quickly than at any time in our history.

So what can you do to stay on track financially? Remember the basics.

As I said at the outset, the traditional approach to personal financial planning focuses on managing wealth — preserving and increasing it. However, unless you have sufficient assets to live comfortably from investment income alone, earning power should continually be given a very high priority. Otherwise, you may not have any wealth to manage.

When we look at the profession of financial planning from this perspective, it may seem that the entire financial services world is barking up the wrong tree, because most people simply don't possess enough wealth to warrant sophisticated asset management strategies. For example, according to the Consumer Federation of America, more than half of American households live from paycheck to paycheck, at least during some of the year. So why do we have a major industry designed to serve a minority of Americans? While there may be more than one simple answer to that question, I'm confident that the approach presented in this book will withstand the test of time.

Historically, when financial planning was an activity reserved solely for the wealthy, focusing on wealth management made perfect sense. In a feudal system, for example, the lord owned everything and everyone; the serfs simply worked until they died in battle protecting their master's territory or succumbed to one of many other perils that kept lifespans far too short for retirement planning.

Once the New World was discovered and the American dream was born, wealthier horizons became visible, but the need for financial planning was still felt by only a small minority. For one thing, the wild nature of the West tended to preempt retirement for many. Then, we invented mass production. No one technically "owned" the people, but some might argue that company towns did a pretty good job of putting a new face on a more benign type of feudal structure, although it did include a company pension.

That was the industrial age, you might say, quite correctly. Now we're in the information age, a time when virtually everyone in this country can finally pursue their own version of the American dream. That's basically true.

We have far more choices than our ancestors, and with these newfound freedoms, we have new responsibilities. Planning our financial lives is key among these. However, sound financial education hasn't reached most of the population yet, and taking the old approach of planning to preserve and build wealth only through saving and smart investing doesn't, by itself, bring about financial security for most people. The traditional get-a-good-education-to-get-a-good-job strategy doesn't suffice, either, because even a doctorate program in an Ivy League college won't necessarily shed much light on how to maximize your earning capacity.

In a business climate where things can change very quickly, it isn't realistic to expect one's income to increase solely on the strength of professional status, job experience or a well-established business. The medical profession is a good example of change eroding financial security. While doctors still earn a good living, many individual practitioners' incomes have been cut by ceilings being imposed on their fees by insurance plans. The rising cost of medical school, combined with declining incomes, has become a deterrent to many would-be doctors in this country, to the point where some medical facilities are forced to recruit new doctors from foreign countries.

So what should you do? Remain vigilant. Keep your eyes and ears open for new opportunities. Stay abreast of business developments that relate to your chosen career, the business sector you work in and other industries where your skills may have value. Get some formal training or on-the-job experience in marketing and sales, regardless of your chosen profession. At the same time, keep increasing your professional knowledge by reading, getting more formal education, participating in professional or business groups — doing whatever you can to grow professionally.

You may be wondering if I'm contradicting myself, because earlier, I noted that income alone doesn't determine how financially secure you become. The fact is, tracking and managing your expenses must have just as high a priority as increasing your earning potential. In other words, the process of managing your money is an ongoing balancing act, juggling dollars in and dollars out.

Along the way, there are many decisions to be made on both sides of the ledger, right down to your choice of a cup of coffee. If you drink a $1.50 brew instead of a $3 version on 333 days of the year, you'll save approximately $1,000 in the course of two years. If that doesn't sound too impressive, consider this: If you charge $1,000 on a credit card with a 17-percent interest rate and pay only minimum payments, it will take 17 years to pay off (assuming you don't use the card again during those years). In that context, the latte just might taste a whole lot better on the 32 other days of the year when you give yourself a treat.

On the income side, let's pretend you have an opportunity to work a few extra hours once or twice a month and earn some extra money, either in your regular job or on another project. However, the work has to be done at the exact time your favorite TV show airs. To complicate matters further, let's pretend you either don't have a VCR or can't figure out how to program it to tape the show in your absence, and asking someone else to tape it for you isn't an option. Yet, that extra money could shave years off a debt. What will you do?

Your decision in that instance and many other, similar ones you face on a day-to-day basis will be driven by your own priorities, which stem from your own personal goals and values. Often, when financial circumstances are not the way we want them to be, our practical choices and goals are not heading in the same direction. To improve matters, one or both have to be adjusted.

Fortunately, that old saying, "Where there's a will, there's a way," is applicable in this case, and it doesn't require advanced degrees to improve one's financial lot. Needless to say, you have to make a plan and follow it. These are some important points to remember to make your financial strategy as effective as possible.

1 | Build a strong foundation.

Know what your goals are; define them clearly. Your own goals are the foundation for all your decisions; the priorities you set and the choices you make should further your aims. For example, when you get a raise or an unexpected windfall, don't go overboard celebrating or throw your plan out the window. Now's the time when you need to stay level-headed and keep your goals in sight. When things look bleak, don't give up on your course to achieve the things that matter to you. If your own goals aren't totally clear at this point, you may want to review the section relating to goals in Chapter 1, as it covers some of the areas you may want to include in planning your future.

2 | Be realistic.

If what you aim for is something you truly want and believe you can achieve, it will be easier to stay motivated. However, even Superman has bad days. Patience and perseverance are always key ingredients of success, and it's easier to exercise both if your goals and your expectations about the time and effort required to achieve them are realistic. You can get into debt very quickly, for example, but it will take a lot longer to dig out.

3 | Be practical.

You can't build a skyscraper with one giant brick. Big things happen as a result of a lot of little things being done again and again for an extended period of time. The actor who seems to gain fame overnight usually worked very hard for years before that moment. We don't become aware of athletes until they step up to the podium to accept their gold medals, but they've been getting out of bed before the crack of dawn to train since they were young children. To win your own "gold," break things down into manageable pieces. Set attainable objectives for income, spending, saving and investing, both for the short and long term. Work out what's most important to do each day and concentrate on doing those things.

4 | Monitor your progress proactively.

The worksheets in the Appendix give a format for planning and tracking both your income and expenses, with "expected" and "actual" amounts. If you are going to take a proactive approach to managing your money, it's important to establish what you expect to make or spend, as well as the actual amounts, and work to turn those expectations into reality. Otherwise, the whole exercise will simply be one of record keeping, rather than a positive process to improve your financial situation.

5 | Exercise creativity.

We tend to think of games as enjoyable activities but ones that are divorced from day-to-day life. Yet the spirit of playing a game is very applicable to problem solving and creating your own financial strategies. If you have a favorite game, whether it's playing or watching a competitive sport or doing a crossword puzzle, try to adopt your "playing" mindset when looking at your own financial picture. Identify the obstacles between the present and the future you envision and enlist your imagination to come up with a good strategy for your own success.

6 | Pay only your fair share in taxes.

Stay out of the trap of thinking a tax refund is a windfall. If you routinely receive more than a small amount, your interest-free loan to the IRS is a liability, even more so if you've been getting a significant refund for many years and you carry debt or have no emergency fund. Those dollars can work much harder for you if you get them sooner. Even if you're squeamish about adjusting your withholding amounts, consult a tax advisor to at least look at your options. And whether you receive a refund or not, ask a competent tax advisor about any possible deductions you may be overlooking. If you rent a home or apartment, find out how spending a comparable amount on mortgage payments would impact your take-home pay.

7 | Be prepared for unforeseen events.

Not having adequate insurance and an emergency fund sets the stage for getting into debt during a crisis. For insurance, see one or more professionals to get a good sense of whether you're adequately covered. You don't want too much or too little. When it comes to emergency funds, there is some consensus that you should pay off high-interest, non-mortgage debt before setting up an emergency fund. However, if you have a track record of getting into debt because of unforeseen expenses or emergencies, it may make more sense for you to put some money aside regardless of debt, as long as you fulfill your payment obligations. Then, you will be less likely to keep using credit repeatedly.

8 | Minimize the cost of credit.

The range of interest rates today is mind boggling, as is the sheer number of credit cards offered to people with just about any type of credit history. In such a credit climate, it's easy to get confused, but some things never change. Often, the better your credit rating, the lower your interest rates, so making timely payments will, in the long run, lower your cost of credit and give you a much bigger choice of lenders. Continuing to make timely payments may keep your rates low. When examining options to transfer debt from one lender to another, you must read the fine print, with no exceptions. Promotional rates are, by definition, temporary. The longer-term rates can take a few extra minutes to find, but they are always disclosed, so look for them and use the best rates available for your needs.

9 | Put your money in smart places.

There isn't one place that's best for everyone's money, and there never will be. There isn't even one type of account or investment that's always best for you. Priorities change with circumstances. Planning to fund a college education for a newborn is quite different from saving to buy a home in five years. The trick is to make your dollars work as hard as possible to perform the most important job for you at any given time — that's the ideal. Since life is usually imperfect, you want to be as smart as possible. If you assign specific functions to chunks of your money, such as paying down debt, saving for a specific purchase or retirement, you can narrow down your options; and the smart places become more obvious.

10 | Keep your eye on the big picture.

If you didn't have to work for a living, what would you really want to do with the rest of your life? Keep in mind that many people who retire early end up going back to some type of work because, after a while, endless golf games lose their appeal, or they miss all their friends who still have to work for a living. Both of those scenarios describe actual people; I didn't make them up. So when you answer the question, try to envision what you would do differently in a typical day, after the novelty of financial independence had worn off. Then, see what you can do, in terms of managing your money, to approach that way of life.

In working with many clients over the years, I've lived through a variety of economic climates and "new" trends. Throughout, I've observed a couple of principles that never change: You always have options. And the choices you make always rest with you.

I hope that the information in this book helps you to see your options more clearly and to make the decisions that are best for you.

Appendix

These worksheets give a format for planning and tracking both your income and expenses, with "expected" and "actual" amounts. Each worksheet contains enough space to track one quarter of the year. You can copy these worksheets and use our format or develop your own, on sheets of paper (filed away safely), in a notebook, in a spreadsheet program or in another format on your computer. How exactly you do it is less important than making sure that you definitely do it. How detailed you get is also up to you. The key thing is to develop a habit of looking at these things on a regular basis — at least once a month.

income tracking worksheet

Income source	Month _____ Expected	Actual	Month _____ Expected	Actual	Month _____ Expected	Actual
Salary						
Commissions						
Bonuses						
Tax refunds						
Child support						
Alimony						
Business or self-employment income						
Dividends						
Interest earned						
Capital gains						
Rent payments						
Trust income						
Social Security						
Pension						
Royalties						
Residuals						
Other						
TOTAL						

Additional information you can track: which sources of income are taxed as ordinary income, which ones are taxed as capital gains, and which ones are not taxed at all. You can use a highlighter or add columns, as needed.

expense tracking worksheet

| Expense | Month _____ | | Month _____ | | Month _____ | |
	Expected	Actual	Expected	Actual	Expected	Actual
Home mortgage or rent						
Second mortgage						
Home equity loan or credit line						
Utilities: electricity						
Utilities: gas						
Utilities: other						
Telephone						
Cable or satellite TV services						
Internet services						
Property taxes						
Homeowners or renters insurance						
Car loan or lease payments						
Car repairs/ maintenance						
Gas						
Toll or other commuting fees						
Insurance: car						
Insurance: health						
Insurance: life						
Insurance: disability						
Insurance: long term care						
Insurance: other						
Clothing						
Medical costs, out of pocket						

expense tracking worksheet _{continued}

Expense	Month _____ Expected	Actual	Month _____ Expected	Actual	Month _____ Expected	Actual
Dental costs						
Groceries						
Dining out						
Other entertainment						
Child care						
School tuition						
College tuition						
Educational costs (other)						
Dry cleaning						
Vacations						
Gifts, including birthdays, anniversaries and Christmas/Chanukah						
Income taxes: federal						
Employment taxes						
Income taxes: state						
Business/other taxes						
Sports or hobbies						
401k or IRA contributions						
Charitable contributions						
Credit card payments						
Other loan payments						
Savings						
Emergency fund						
Other						
TOTAL						

Additional information you can track: expenses that are tax deductible from federal and/or state taxes and whether 100 percent or a smaller percentage of an expense is deductible. You can also track which expenses will earn interest and how much, and how much interest you are paying on debt. You can use a highlighter or add columns, as needed.

give the gift of

A Step-by-Step Guide to
Financial
Bli$$

Visit your local bookstore
or call
800-247-6553

Free Shipping
on orders of
2 or more copies

Discounts
on phone orders of
5 or more copies

For online orders:
www.guidetobliss.com

www.ingramcontent.com/pod-product-compliance
Lightning Source LLC
Chambersburg PA
CBHW031928190326
41519CB00007B/453